THE CHURCH BEYOND THE CHURCH

THE CHURCH BEYOND THE CHURCH

Sheffield Industrial Mission 1944-1994

Paul Bagshaw

with a foreword by
The Right Reverend David Sheppard
Bishop of Liverpool

First published 1994

A catalogue record for this book is available from the British Library.

ISBN 0-9522860-0-9

Industrial Mission in South Yorkshire
IMSY Centre
Cemetery Road Baptist Church
Sheffield S11 8HA

Printed in Great Britain by Sheffield Design & Print
740 Staniforth Road, Sheffield S9 3GY

For Hilly, Joanna, and Anthony

Contents

ILLUSTRATIONS

1. Scott Paradise with furnace bricklayers; Steel, Peech and Tozer, 1956.

2. Steelworkers' Conference at William Temple College, Rugby. Ted Wickham, front row left.

3. Michael Jackson with railway workers at Darnall Locomotive sheds, 1959.

4. Margaret Kane in the lorry garage at Firth Brown, 1965.

between pages 30 and 31

5. Harry Cole visiting Spear and Jackson, 1969.

6. The Provost of Sheffield Cathedral, the Very Revd Frank Curtis, Mrs Fanny Mudia and the Rt Revd James Mudia, Bishop of Maseno North, Kenya, visiting a steel works with Malcolm Grundy.

7. One of the highlights of the annual Theological Students' course is an underground pit visit, here at Houghton Main in July, 1992.

8. The IMSY staff in 1994. *(left to right)* John Kenward, Roy Newell, Norman Young, Barry Parker, Elizabeth Nash, Margaret Halsey, Mike West, Tony Attwood, Chris Sissons.

between pages 80 and 81

Foreword

I am pleased to commend *The Church Beyond the Church*, not only for Paul Bagshaw's intriguing history of Sheffield Industrial Mission, but also because it reveals some of the opportunities and constraints facing the Christian Church endeavouring to minister within the world of work.

Life is sustained by the daily work of millions of people. This economic process not only provides for material needs of individuals and communities, but also bears heavily upon the spiritual quality of life. Christians believe that the love and justice of God encompasses the whole economic order: so the mission and ministry of the Church is engaged with the world of work, both corporately through its structures, and individually with those who work or seek work.

Ever since 1944, when Bishop Leslie Hunter appointed Ted Wickham to pioneer a ministry within the steel industry, Sheffield Industrial Mission has maintained a dynamic and determined Christian presence within the economic life of South Yorkshire. *The Church Beyond the Church* narrates the history of this courageous, and sometimes controversial, Christian endeavour from 1944 to 1994. Paul Bagshaw's work will interest not only the people of Sheffield, but many others who have struggled to understand, in the light of the Christian gospel, the forces at work within industrial society, to offer an appropriate ministry to people with and without employment, and to determine the will of God for the Church within the economic order.

In the 1960s there was major conflict within the Sheffield Industrial Mission, involving a clash between different theologies and approaches. It is difficult to represent each point of view with equal weight, but Paul Bagshaw has researched thoroughly, seeking to hold the scales fairly between different accounts. It is a witness to the value of industrial mission that after all the pain of those years, the Sheffield Industrial Mission has found fresh and renewed ways of working in God's world.

At different times this mission field has been regarded as a gulf, across which industrial mission has dared to step, or as a frontier at which the Church meets the world of every day. At a time in European history when market forces liberate some and exclude others, when technological change is both feared and acclaimed, and when the Future of Work is regarded as one of the most pressing issues of out time, the love and justice of God must, more than ever, be known and understood, not just within the Church, but throughout the created order.

I commend to you not only this book, but the whole ecumenical mission of the Church 'beyond the Church' in which Sheffield has played a leading role for the past fifty years.

The Right Reverend David Sheppard
Bishop of Liverpool
Chairman, Board for Social Responsibility of the General Synod of the Church of England

PREFACE

Mission in the Church's Back Yard

Sheffield Industrial Mission was born in April 1944 when Ted Wickham was appointed Industrial Chaplain in the Diocese of Sheffield. This was an innovative and at the time unique appointment. It was created by the Bishop of Sheffield, Dr Leslie Hunter, to further his vision of a revitalised Church and a Church re-established amongst the industrial working class. There was no guarantee of success, but Wickham took up Hunter's challenge with acuity and enthusiasm. The mission that he founded proved that the Church could be embedded in industry. The following years saw the near destruction of Wickham's mission, but it survived, though rebuilt on fundamentally different principles. In 1990 it was renamed Industrial Mission in South Yorkshire. It was an experiment that succeeded.

1994 sees SIM's Golden Jubilee. A 50th birthday is a time to celebrate, to take stock, and to look to the future. This book contributes to all three. The story is worth the telling for its own sake, and it is also an opportunity to examine how the Christian missionary imperative has been worked out in practice and in theory in a secular, industrial context in the Church's own back yard.

The 50 years since the Second World War have been characterised by unprecedented change in every aspect of life. The industry in which the Mission works has been altered almost beyond recognition. In 1944, when Wickham came to Sheffield, the steel and engineering industries dominated the whole of Sheffield physically and economically. Vast works employed thousands of men pouring out and working steel for the war effort. In 1994 most of these works have vanished. Some have been replaced by sports facilities and shopping centres. Some are now only fields of rubble. Those manufacturing companies that survived use processes and equipment undreamed of in 1944, and they employ only a small fraction of the people they once needed.

The face of South Yorkshire has changed. Slum clearance and new housing estates have changed the appearance of the county, not just in the urban centres of Sheffield, Rotherham, Barnsley[1] and Doncaster, but also in the surrounding agricultural and mining villages. Social change has accompanied physical change. In 1944 the Beveridge Report and the prospect of a welfare state were matters of heated discussion, not least amongst the forces still fighting the war across Europe and the Far East. In 1994 the dismantling of the welfare state can still occasionally arouse passion, but is more often met with resignation.

The Church too has changed. Its numbers and influence have steadily declined. Yet at the same time liturgical reform, the ecumenical movement, and vigorous theological debate have given Churches a progressively more relaxed and open culture since the 1960s, though introspective and clerical pressures have never been absent. Change has also been imposed on the Church, not least by the economic and political developments of the 1980s which forced Churches to re-evaluate their relationship with the secular world, and pushed the Church of England in particular to reassess its relationship with the State.

Sheffield Industrial Mission was an Anglican creation, and this has coloured the whole of its history and thinking including, until recently, its approach to ecumenism. Similarly the Mission's action and reflection in the sphere of politics has been undertaken against the background of the established Church and its relationship to the State. SIM is an agency of the Church, and the overall relationship between the Church and the political world both gives the Mission opportunities, and limits what it can do. As that prior relationship has changed, so too has the capacity for SIM to involve itself in political issues.

This history follows a roughly chronological pattern, divided according to the tenures of successive Senior Chaplains. A little of the background which led Bishop Hunter to invite Wickham to the Diocese is set out in Chapter 1. Chapter 2 follows Wickham's creation and nurturing of the Mission. The subsequent development of the Mission on modified lines under Michael Jackson's leadership in the 1960s, and its abrupt and traumatic change of direction, are outlined in Chapter 3. Chapter 4 describes SIM's steady reconstruction through the 1970s, led by Andrew Stokes, Malcolm Grundy, and Raymond Draper. Chapter 5, the 1980s, surveys SIM's search under Mike West for new ways of working in the face of the widespread devastation of industry, and the arrival of new patterns of employment.

The chronological thread is interrupted by Chapter 6. This traces SIM's relationship with the coal mining industry. In doing so it also traces a major shift in the relationship of the Church to the secular world. In 1944 the Church was in part financially dependent on the mining industry; in 1993 it was lobbying the Government on behalf of the industry, but from a position of critical independence. Chapter 7 looks at the Mission between 1990 and 1993. However this brings the story far too close to the present be able to make any kind of historical judgement.

The bulk of the book is concerned with the celebration and stock taking appropriate to a 50th birthday. For the whole of its life SIM has been a sustained practical experiment of contemporary mission, working out the Christian faith in the changing secular, industrial world. The experiment has at times followed sharply divergent paths, but throughout its history the Mission has struggled to bridge the gap between the transformatory potential of Christian faith and the doggedly mundane realities of everyday life. The postscript uses the linked ideas of the "gulf" and the "frontier" to analyse the changing experiment. It also draws out some of the dominant themes which have arisen in the course of the history of Sheffield Industrial Mission.

Thanks are due to a great number of people who have helped in the preparation of this account, and especially to those who gave generously of their time to recall for me their part in the Mission. Apologies are due to all those I was not able to see and whose contribution to the mission is alluded to only briefly or not at all. Sadly it did not prove possible to meet and talk about the Mission with its founder, Bishop Wickham. Particular thanks are due to Dr John Atherton, and to Mike West and the Industrial Mission Council who commissioned the history and who encouraged and supported me in its preparation. Responsibility for errors, omissions, and misjudgements, however, remains entirely mine.

NOTES

1. Barnsley lies in the Diocese of Wakefield and only comes into this story briefly in the 1980s.

1

War, Steel, and the Challenge of Sheffield

"Oh no! *Not* Sheffield!"

Grace Hunter spoke for them both. Her husband, Leslie Stannard Hunter, was Archdeacon of Northumberland. He had every expectation of becoming a bishop, but he was not delighted by the letter from the Prime Minister, Neville Chamberlain, which offered him the see of Sheffield. Nonetheless, after some persuasion, he accepted.[1] The Hunters arrived in Sheffield in September 1939.

Leslie Hunter was a short man with no small talk. Balding at the front, with sharp eyes and an incisive mind he intimidated some and inspired life-long admiration in others. He was a visionary, an administrator, and he could be thoroughly devious in getting his way. He supported women's ministry, encouraged worship as a thing of beauty, and campaigned for the reform of the financial structures of the Church of England. He promoted Moral Welfare and Social Responsibility work. He built links with churches in Scandinavia, in Europe and with the nascent World Council of Churches. In all his commitments he held together in himself the two dimensions of discipleship, the temporal and the transcendent. Mission and worship were inseparable.

In his theology and in his action Hunter stood midstream in the history of Anglican social Christianity. After Oxford he had worked for the Student Christian Movement. While there he participated in an interdenominational enquiry into the religious faith and practice of the ordinary soldiery in the First World War. In 1919 it published its report, *The Army and Religion*, spelling out the gulf that lay between the Church and the working class soldiers. In a retirement speech in 1962, over 40 years later, Hunter traced his concern for mission to the working class back to the impact of this enquiry.

In 1924, then Canon at Newcastle Cathedral, Hunter took part in the interdenominational Conference on Politics, Economics and Citizenship (COPEC). The conference had been carefully prepared, and under the leadership of William Temple it provided a focus and a rallying cry for socially minded Christians, and it explored some of the social implications of the Gospel for the issues of the day. On his return Hunter convened a further conference, Northern COPEC. This gathering led to the commissioning of a detailed and lucid survey of industrial life in the area,[2] the foundation of the Social Council for Tyneside (later the Newcastle Council for Voluntary Service), and a great deal of practical work ameliorating the worst effects of the depression and the general strike. After a short spell as Vicar of Barking, where he was actively involved in campaigning for better housing, smoke abatement, and better provision for the unemployed, Hunter returned to Newcastle, this time as Archdeacon. There he became chairman of the Social Council for Tyneside, working to provide practical help for the unemployed, and encouraging his clergy to see their role in a social context.[3]

When he moved to Sheffield Hunter was not impressed by the diocese he had inherited. He rapidly formed a low opinion of the quality of the clergy and of their failure to address the needs of their great industrial region. Church buildings existed in the industrial areas of the Diocese, blackened like everything else by the smog, but the inside of industry was foreign territory to the Church. This was an indictment, but not a crisis. The Diocese had always valued its links with individual industrialists, but it had never been strong in Sheffield's working class districts. Nor did the Diocese play any significant part in civic affairs which were dominated by trades unions and the Labour Party. If anything, its political sympathies lay the other side of the fence with the Conservative establishment.

Hunter's immediate priority, however, was to respond to the exigencies of war. The Church shared the national combination of upheaval, destruction, and business as normal. Churches and clergy were tipped out of their stable routines, garden fetes and bazaars were cancelled, and evening services stopped because few churches could satisfy blackout requirements. Thirteen of the diocese's clergy were absent with the forces. Sheffield suffered badly in the blitz of December 1940. Amongst the devastation were 12 churches and 40 vicarages damaged, and six churches destroyed. During the same period Hunter found time to reorganise the Diocese's finances, restructure the deaneries and several of the parishes, and to begin to make overtures to local industrialists and trades unionists.

War proved kind to industrial mission. Some parish priests, alongside fire watching and ARP duties, took the opportunity to visit local factories as part of their pastoral responsibilities. War also generated a strong ethos of common purpose. Business competitors sank their rivalry for the duration, and worked together for the war effort. Conflict between workers and management was pushed into second place. In addition, many working men had contact with forces padres which contributed to the acceptance of padres in the works. The very destruction, social disruption, and sacrifice of war gave many the conviction that a new world was both necessary and possible. The election of the Labour government in 1945 made it a reality.

From his arrival in Sheffield, Hunter was concerned to build connections with industry, and in particular with the industrial working class. He discovered few Christian lay people active on the shop floor of industry. His own early attempts to contact trades-union leaders were rebuffed. One symbolic incident stuck in his memory:

> "When the Trades and Labour Council was invited to be officially present at a service [on Industry Sunday, April 26th, 1942] at which William Temple, shortly after he went to Canterbury, was to speak, the invitation was accepted only after a sharp difference of opinion on the Council, and it was the first time it had done such a thing. This was indicative of a gap and a depth of suspicion which one had not met on Tyneside or in the mining communities of the North-east."[4]

Hunter's vision of what the Church needed to do was based on his analysis of the gap between the Church and the working class. He did not seek to minimise the challenge that faced him.

Sociologically, churchgoing was predominantly a middle-class activity which scarcely touched the working class. Politically, the preponderance of liberal or conservative churchgoers stood in opposition to the trades-union based socialism dominant in the works. Culturally, the everyday life of most clergy and congregations and that of the shop-floor worker were alien worlds to one another. Religiously, a chasm lay between the spiritual claims of faith and the unthinking secularism of the majority.

Hunter held the Church itself largely responsible for the divorce with secular society. It had failed to respond to the Enlightenment and to other developments which had contributed to the divide.

> "Because Churchmen were wanting in courage and insight an industrial society grew up in many countries which was little girded by Christian principle. It was careless about justice; it gave no thought to the spirituality of physical work; it treated man as a means to material ends. Therefore this industrial society became a secular society in which the increasing population crowded together under bad living conditions were rootless and unquiet."[5]

The failure was still present. For the whole of his life Hunter remained deeply critical of the complacency of the Church and its wilful refusal to take seriously its missionary task. Few saw the urgency and profundity of the challenge as he did.

But the challenge was immense and vitally urgent. The character of the social revolution which was expected to follow the ending of the war would threaten the continued existence of the Church of England. The new age, many believed, would be the "Age of the Common Man". Society would be organised in the interests of the working class, and not for the old elite. But the Church of England was visibly aligned with the capitalists and alienated from the Common Man. Unless a bridge could rapidly and effectively be built between it and the working class, the Church was in real danger of being discarded.

Hunter's analysis went still further. He perceived post-war society to be a wholly new phenomenon. He believed that industry was not simply economically dominant, but that, for the first time, it *determined* the nature of society, politically, culturally and even spiritually. Consequently, he argued, if Christianity was not embedded in the very heart of the new industrial culture, then a bleak, amoral, superficial secularism would thrive. The action (or inaction) of the Church at this turning point of history was of paramount importance to its future. The stakes were the highest: on the one hand the very survival of the Church, and on the other the opportunity to shape the whole character of society in a Christian manner.

It was clear that the Church's old methods had failed, and were inadequate to the modern task. New and radical measures, sufficient to "look forward to a new order both in Church and society",[6] would be needed to bridge the gap. By 1943 Hunter had begun to look for someone with the experience and the ability to address the challenge.

NOTES

1. *Strategist for the Spirit – Leslie Hunter, Bishop of Sheffield 1939-1962*, G. Hewitt (ed.), Becket Publications, 1985, p.61

2. *Industrial Tyneside*, Henry Mess, Ernest Benn, 1928. The work was originally published in 2d pamphlets as each section was completed.

3. see: "The Church in its Industrial Setting", Peter Dodd; and "Social Work in the Diocese", Kathleen Lloyd; in: *A Social History of the Diocese of Newcastle*, W.S.F. Pickering (ed.), Oriel Press, 1981; and G. Hewitt, op. cit.

4. *A Mission of the People of God, being a Picture of an English Diocese and a Visitation Charge in AD 1960*, L.S. Hunter, SPCK, 1961, p.18

5. "The Church and Industrial Society, A Sermon delivered in the Cathedral of Nidaros, Trondheim, Norway", L.S. Hunter, *Sheffield Diocesan Review,* December 1952.

6. "Evangelism", L.S. Hunter, *Sheffield Diocesan Review*, November 1941.

2

New Expressions of the Church, 1944-1959

1944-1949, Brilliant improvisations

Hunter was an opportunist. He knew what he wanted, and to attain it he would use whatever means came to hand. In 1944 a vacancy arose for a Chaplain and Governor of the Shrewsbury Hospital (almshouses which form part of the Duke of Norfolk's estate). In the straitened circumstances of war-time Hunter presented the Hospital trustees with a choice. They could have no chaplain at all; or they could appoint Ted Wickham half time, on condition that he be the Bishop's "industrial padre" for the other half. The trustees acquiesced and Hunter thus instigated what was to become the Sheffield Industrial Mission.

Edward Ralph (Ted) Wickham had worked in the plastics industry before training for the priesthood at St Stephen's House, Oxford. He was ordained in 1938 at the age of 27. He served as a curate in Newcastle, briefly overlapping with Hunter, and in 1941 he became Chaplain to some 25,000 people at Royal Ordnance Factory No. 5 at Swynnerton, in the Diocese of Lichfield. He was already being noticed: the Student Christian Movement hoped to appoint him as their Industrial Secretary and successor to Edwin Barker, but Hunter snapped him up first.

Wickham's initial brief was to experiment and to explore. He was

"to find out by trial in the next two years whether there might be a full-time job for a man with his experience on the shop floors of the big steel works if managers and men invited him."[1]

Hunter later described Wickham's work in this period as a series of brilliant improvisations. The right man and the right conditions came together. The experiment worked.

Wickham was a charismatic cockney. He enjoyed outdoor activities, caving, rock climbing, fishing. He was a serious mountaineer which indicated, he thought, certain characteristics: resilience, determination, and perhaps even a certain arrogance. On the other hand he kept birds – budgerigars and parakeets – which would fly around the room and settle on his head during conversations, evoking pastoral images of St Francis. On the shop floor he would peer over his spectacles and engage people in animated discussion on almost any topic. He would pick up a point and push disputants to clarify their views in a manner which brought out the best in them. Some nicknamed him "cannonball" because of the impact he made. He would gather a group around him for the kind of heated discussion that includes everyone and provokes both thought and further debate. He was a man with a mission, a message. He would convince any who would listen – workers, managers, clergy, laity – of the serious claims of a modern Christianity. In the works he attracted widespread admiration and respect.

Church agencies had experience of work with industry upon which Wickham could potentially draw. The most consistent Christian work had been undertaken by the Industrial Christian Fellowship whose missionaries had worked in a number of industries, including the First World War ordnance factories. Between the wars its General Secretary, P.T.R. Kirk, had been deeply involved in Anglican social Christianity, yet by the 1940s the ICF had lost both momentum and standing. There was also periodic evangelistic interest in industrial workers. The "Christian Commandos", for example, mounted two-week crusades on factory workers in Nottingham, Reading and elsewhere. These raids would now be forgotten but for their association with the Methodist Minister Bill Gowland who later founded the Luton Industrial College. Wickham dismissed all such evangelistic approaches as totally inadequate.

There had also been local initiatives in Sheffield. In the early 1940s, Hunter frequently exhorted the parochial clergy to develop new ways of working with industry. In 1941 Richard Roseveare (later Bishop of Accra) established a branch of the Young Christian Workers.[2] The group stressed the dignity of work. Through a method summarised as "See, Judge, Act" they sought to train young working-class Christians to be effective missionaries and apostles at their work place.

Other diocesan activity in relation to industry continued alongside Wickham's work. Archdeacon Stannard, for example, had links with a number of companies in Doncaster. In November 1946 he organised a "Works Leadership Week" on the model of the Moral Leadership Courses run by forces chaplains. Four firms sent six men each for a week of lectures and discussions on Christianity and its relevance to industry. It showed both that firms were prepared to allow workers to attend courses organised by the Church during the working week, and also that non-Christian workers were prepared to attend. In Sheffield, the Moral Welfare worker, Miss Blackburn, went into industry to lecture large groups of young women on matters of sexuality and morality. Personal interviews were also available. In the

Bishop's Letter of December 1945 Blackburn is said to be working under the industrial chaplain; in January 1946 this was corrected: she was working under the Bishop and "co-operating" with the industrial chaplain.

In addition to the war-time opportunist visiting of factories, there were also examples of more systematic programmes of works visiting. In Bristol a Baptist, C.H.Cleal, worked in five factories building up small cells of Christians to help them explore the relevance of their faith in their work. In London Cuthbert Bardsley had begun visiting Siemens Brothers, an underground electrical factory in Woolwich. He established a "quiet room" with an altar in the factory and held regular lunch-time services. A full-time chaplaincy in a large paper-mill in Fife was described in the *Christian News-Letter* of July 1943.

None of these was sufficient. The challenge Hunter had set Wickham was not just whether he could find techniques for talking to working-class men, but whether he could bridge the yawning gulf between the Church and the industrial working class. This was far more than extending Church activity or presence into an unaccustomed field. It was a mission into territory which was alien to the Church and alienated from the Church. It demanded both new methods and new theology.

There was one other initiative which regarded the gulf with equal seriousness, and which was much more than an extension of existing Church activity. The French Worker-Priest movement was similarly a combination of new methods and new theological thinking.[3] Careful sociological study in the 1930s had revealed that the proletariat masses were almost completely alienated from the Catholic Church, that anti-clericalism was rife, and that much of life was utterly secular. In Paris, Cardinal Suhard decided to take radical measures to face the challenge. In 1942 the *Mission de France* seminary was opened, and the *Mission de Paris* in 1943. They were created to provide priests trained and willing to work in the toughest and most alienated working-class districts of the country and the capital; training included a year or two of factory work.

The pressures on the French Church under German occupation were immense. Cardinal Suhard was exercised about the spiritual care of French workers deported to Germany as forced labour. The German authorities refused the Church permission to accompany the workers. Suhard sent 25 French priests disguised as workers alongside the labourers. All but one were unmasked and shot. Henri Perrin, the survivor, published his diary and reflections which were rapidly translated into English.[4]

The experience of the war and urban missions convinced Cardinal Suhard and others that the experiment could succeed. The young priests who joined the movement discarded the outward trappings of conventional ministry, and began to discover a new priesthood in identification with the proletariat. They entered fully into the working-class milieu, trades unionism (the communist CGT, not the Catholic CFTC), and the industrial works. They concealed their ordination, only revealing it if asked. There was no shortage of volunteers to join the new order of priest-workmen.

After the war active and personal links were quickly established between Wickham and the *Mission de Paris*. Wickham met some of the leaders of the worker-priest movement in Paris in 1949, and several of them visited Sheffield. Mutual respect, however, could not disguise fundamental differences of approach, and in the mid-1950s these became a public dispute (see below, p.39).

But as early as 1945 the Vatican expressed its unease. At first employers had applied to bishops for such conscientious and stabilising workers. But post-war France grew steadily more polarised and several of the priests were increasingly and visibly involved in left-wing politics. Some participated in pitched battles with the police in the context of industrial disputes, and in conflict with the State on the welfare of immigrant workers. Employers changed their tune. They grew to fear such well trained and dedicated union leaders and complained about them to both the police and the Church hierarchy. The Vatican shutters started to come down. In 1947 the cold war began in earnest, and in 1949 the Vatican issued the "Decree against Communism", banning all collaboration between Catholics and communists. The French hierarchy interpreted the decree with a certain broad-mindedness, but Rome progressively curtailed the freedom of the worker-priests until, in September 1953, Pius XII abolished the movement in France. Bishop Hunter was in Rome and had been due to meet Cardinal Suhard the day the announcement was made.[5]

In Sheffield, in the daunting conditions of steel manufacture, Wickham went about his mission with a personal, unique style. The only significance he gave to most other national and local approaches was to contrast them with his own. Steel makers were vast employers by modern standards. There was full employment in the 1940s first to arm and armour the forces and then to feed reconstruction. The trade union movement was strong. Production was all important. Much shop-floor work consisted of bursts of intense and concentrated activity, interspersed with slack periods which proved ideal for informal gatherings. The reduction in the endemic antagonism of management and workers continued after the war, though conflict was never wholly removed. In this new world ideals of consensus and common purpose, at least as goals, were popular. Britain had pulled together during the war, and the early years of the welfare state showed it could also pull together for the common good in peace time. Wickham's message resonated with this ethos.

There were distractions. Wickham was first asked to be padre to 500 "Bevin boys" (miners organised by the Ministry of Labour during the war) who were housed in nine hostels across the Diocese, a task he quickly passed on. In 1948 six Labour MPs, including the maverick radical Richard Acland, decided to hold a mission and chose Sheffield as their target city. They were deflected into a busy week with Wickham and emerged convinced of the value of industrial mission and of the need for sustained and properly resourced work in industry. In 1949 Hunter sent Wickham and two other clergy from the Diocese to participate in the large scale Mission to London.

But most of Wickham's time was spent in the muck and noise of Sheffield's steel industry. There he rose to the challenge Hunter had set him and created the "Sheffield model" of factory visiting. Its basic strategy and ground rules were established in the first few months of his appointment. There were initially four aspects to the Sheffield model: negotiating access; visiting; "snap-break" (sandwich or meal break) meetings; and taking debate further.

An initial approach to a company might come after contact with individuals in either the trades unions or management. But from the start it was a cardinal rule that formal access was negotiated with both sides of industry in order to avoid the identification of the chaplain with either. In the first place Wickham relied on Hunter's contacts with the company's management.

Wickham's first chaplaincy was in Firth Vickers Stainless. His arrival in 1944 was preceded by a memorandum sent around the company by its Managing Director, Mr C.E. (Eric) Holstrom, a member of the Church Burgesses[6] and a long-term supporter of industrial mission. The memo announced that a member of the Church of England clergy would be coming round the firm, and that his sole aim was to try to relate Christianity to industry.

Once inside a company Wickham would wander around talking to individuals and working groups. This regular, sustained, undramatic visiting was the foundation stone of all other industrial mission activity. In this way he got to know the men, the managers, the activists and the issues in each part of the works. Wickham never forgot he was there on sufferance. All new chaplains had it drummed into them that they were guests in industry and they must not get in the way of the primary purpose of the works: to make steel.

Wickham was not everyone's idea of a vicar, and this was to his advantage:

"I met Ted Wickham and I got rather a shock. [He was] a tousle haired, smallish man, iron grey, glasses, and he talked straight at you, thump! And straight away I thought, 'I like this bloke. He'll have a go, one way and another', and believe you me he had to have a go, because of the questions that were asked him. 'What's tha come for?' this was the first question. And he tried to explain that he thought that there was a relationship between industry and Christianity. But the question arose 'Well why have you suddenly started now?' After all the workers went through during the depression and at the turn of the century, and during the industrial revolution, and building the slums and all, why didn't the Church do something then?"[7]

Wherever possible Wickham would set up an informal, "snap break", gathering for discussion and argument. Anywhere between 20 and 100 people would join in. They would sit around him on boxes or propped up against the machines in a convenient corner, or around the tables in the cabin where they took their breaks (there were few works canteens in the 1940s). Some would use the opportunity for a smoke. For 15 or 20 minutes there would be animated debate which would frequently be continued later on the shop floor or going home on the bus. Snap-break meetings became the hallmark of the Sheffield model.

Wickham was quick witted, well read, and more than a match for shop-floor debaters, but his objective was not to defeat them nor to persuade them. His task was to get them hooked. As he went round he would also identify those who might develop a deeper interest in Christianity. There was never enough time to go into any depth of discussion in the works, and two of the groups that Wickham had set up in Firth Vickers, a staff group of both men and women, and a shop-floor group, decided that they would like to go deeper into what Wickham was saying. They arranged to meet Wickham on Thursday evenings at his home. It was still wartime, the blackout was in force, and the journey itself could be memorable. The group met weekly for theological discussion and Bible study. After a while, and at the request of group members, a short informal service was held in the Chapel of the Shrewsbury Hospital as part of the meeting. Some of the group were later confirmed into the Church of England.

By 1946 it was decided to change the character of the group. It became an open group with invitations issued to the families, friends, and neighbours of members, and a particular welcome was extended to demobilised soldiers. It was renamed the "Peoples' Discussion Group" and focused on the problems and challenges of post-war society. By the end of the year it had become too big for Wickham's house. In January 1947 the meeting moved to Room No. 1 of Church House and a small sub-committee was set up to administer the meeting. A bank account was opened, leaflets were printed to announce the programme of meetings, and occasional advertisements were placed in the local paper. There was a small circulating library. There were social evenings, coach trips to the sea-side, social weekends at Hollowford near Castleton, and an annual Christmas party.

The group continued to evolve. In 1948/49 they again reviewed progress. They concluded that an open discussion meeting was good for bringing people into the mission, but not good at keeping them, nor at going further into the Christian faith. They decided to add a second meeting, on a Sunday evening, for those who wished to go deeper into Christianity. This was called the "Faith and Fellowship Movement". It was aimed at lay believers who kept one foot in the Church and one foot in the world, and comprised a short and simple service of worship and discussion about the Christian faith.

Notwithstanding Wickham's welcome in the works and the response of some to the Christian faith, the gulf between the Church and the industrial working class was still strong. It was reflected in suspicion, misunderstandings, and prejudice on both sides. This had to be tackled first before any substantive initiative could be taken. By entering the works Wickham was off Church territory; in raising religious issues he was also off industrial territory. It was unthreatening – people assumed that a churchman would simply want to recruit them, or to take their money, or to stop them drinking, swearing, and enjoying sex. Many distinguished the Church from Christianity and both criticism of the Church, and respect for Christianity were frequent starting points for discussion. Wickham's openness and willingness to go out to people created the conditions for lively and sometimes deep discussions.

Part of the gulf also reflected male working-class culture. Church was seen as women's territory, and many men would not be seen entering a Church building. Women, on the other hand, could be reached by parish clergy because they were more often at home. Hunter was particularly concerned that the mission addressed the men, though women workers were not to be neglected.

Part of the gulf was political. Trades-union culture was strong and many people saw the Church as aligned with their capitalist enemies, a view which was not without evidence. Alternatively, many clergy appeared to regard the whole idea of politics with distaste, and Church life was often a world away from people who were politically active. Wickham avoided partisan political allegiance, though he relished political issues.

As Wickham's reputation spread, the work he was asked to do increased and he began to visit an increasing number of companies. In 1948 Leslie Hayes was appointed as Wickham's first "assistant Industrial Padre" and the first full-time missioner. The work was paid for out of the "Church in Action – War Emergency Fund". This was a subscription fund set up in March 1945, primarily for rebuilding churches in the Diocese that had been damaged during the war. Ten per cent of the fund was earmarked for training, and there seems to have been little constraint on how the Bishop used this money. In Samuel Fox & Co. money had been raised by deducting 1*d* or.2*d* per week from the workers' wages. Sheffield Industrial Mission was known as "The Church in Action" in this company for many years because of this association.

Money was always a touchy point. In 1948 Hunter expressed the hope that firms and workers would fund more chaplains, though in retirement he observed that it would have been fatal had management paid chaplains directly, or be thought to have done so.[8] Nonetheless, considerable if indirect financial support by companies for chaplains was present from the beginning.

Another key question from the start of the Mission was the relationship of its work with the rest of the Church. Officially, the Mission addressed industrial communities, complementing the parishes which addressed geographic communities. Yet Wickham's critique of the parochial structure of the Church was fundamental and scarcely veiled: the Church was imprisoned in the middle classes; its theology was wholly inadequate to the missionary task it faced; its parochial organisation was quite insufficient for the social structures of the second half of the twentieth century. Parish Churches were very largely complacent, introspective, and uninterested in changing. Industrial mission was the advancing front; parish work was the "back lines". Not surprisingly many parish clergy took this criticism personally and from some Wickham evoked considerable antipathy.

Hunter's initial conception was that Wickham would create a "bridgehead" in industry: a secure landing point through which Christian laity could invade, liberating the workers from the spiritually debilitating effects of secularism. Very quickly the two men were agreed that this hope underestimated the extent of the divide between the Church and the industrial working class, and overvalued the capacity of Christians for mission. Industrial workers could not be simply "drafted" into the Church, they would not go; and few Churches were sufficiently Christ-centred to be able to reach out effectively to the workers.

Therefore Hunter agreed to Wickham's proposal to try something different, an experiment that would be a radical departure from the customary, parochial ordering of the Church of England. Workers associated with the Mission were to be formed into groups which would remain outside the parish structure, at least for the foreseeable future. They would become a church outside the Church. The sole connecting point with the institutional Church would be the Mission, or perhaps even Wickham himself. Instead of trying to bring the Church and the working class together, Wickham worked to bring Christianity to the working class. Instead of the bridgehead, SIM was to be the bridge between Church and industry: a narrow point of contact keeping both sides apart.

Training was a key element of the relationship between industrial mission and the Church. If the Mission was to grow, and especially if its experience and approach were to be promulgated outside Sheffield, it was important to ensure a supply of chaplains trained, able, and willing to take on the work. In June 1949 Hunter convened a conference at Sheffield University with a number of his fellow Bishops and the Church's Advisory Council on Training for Ministry (CACTM). He proposed a pattern of training which would equip ordinands for ministry in an industrial world by giving them supervised experience of shop-floor work. It was a hot day, and the bishops in their braces decided to give Hunter's proposals further thought.

Hunter kept very close watch on the development of the Mission through regular meetings with Wickham and Hayes. He periodically convened informal and private meetings of industrialists and, separately, of trades unionists. These gatherings were aimed at building better relations between the Church and industry, and in particular between the Church and labour. They also served to inform Hunter of the opinions those on the receiving end held of the Mission. In 1949 Hunter formally reviewed the Mission. He had decided it was a success long before; the "review" was designed to command support for its expansion. A meeting of 142 industrialists convened by the Master Cutler[9] agreed on the need for the urgent expansion of the Mission's work and committed themselves to support it, not least financially. The following day a meeting of trades-union officials offered their goodwill and critical support to the mission.

Wickham had met Hunter's challenge. He had shown that there was a welcome for a padre in the steel works. He had proved that the industrial working class, whom Hunter felt to be so estranged from the Church, would respond positively and actively to a strong presentation of a lively, relevant, attractive Christianity. He had laid down the foundations on which industrial mission could be constructed. It was set to enter a new phase with the new decade.

1950-1954 The Mission established

In 1950 Sheffield Industrial Mission ceased to be an experiment and took permanent shape.

In March that year Ted Wickham left the Shrewsbury Hospital. He was made a Residentiary Canon of Sheffield Cathedral to permit him to devote his whole attention to the Mission. An Industrial Mission Advisory Committee was established with representation from management, the trades-union movement, and clergy outside the Mission. It was strictly advisory, and not expected to constrain either Hunter's or Wickham's freedom of action, but its presence acknowledged the legitimate involvement of both sides of industry in SIM's affairs. Bishop Hunter was proud of this committee. It was the only place of which he was aware where management and workers sat down together on the same side of the table, a tangible sign of industrial reconciliation.

A prime reason for the formation of the Advisory Committee was the need to formalise SIM's finances as it expanded. At Samuel Fox workers continued to make small donations from their wages: by the end of 1951 a total of 1,575 people, over a quarter of the work force, contributed. They were joined by workers at the Stocksbridge Railway Company. Of a total income of £1,650 in 1951, giving from companies and employees constituted 52%; the Church 40%; and the remainder came from investments held by the Bishop. By 1954 the equivalent proportions were: industry 65%, the Church 24%, and 10% from interest and reimbursement of salaries, with a total income of £2,677. The Mission had also begun to accumulate reserves of its own.

Staff numbers grew steadily. In 1950 there were two full-time chaplains. Leslie Hayes left in 1951 and was replaced by Michael Brooke. Philip Bloy joined in 1952, and the first woman chaplain, Kay Hancock[10] in 1953. Scott Paradise arrived in 1954. As numbers grew so the work could expand.

Hunter kept in very close touch with developments. He met with Wickham most weeks. Every month he celebrated Holy Communion with the team, and had breakfast with them. This was an opportunity for informal discussion with the team, without Wickham, and the chance to talk to chaplains individually. Hunter had a deep pastoral concern for missioners doing often lonely work. He was also clear about the need for the Church to exercise its authority over its agency. On occasions Hunter could be directive: for example, he instructed that the Mission's monthly Holy Communion should move from Church House and be held in the Cathedral. Or he would present Wickham with a *fait accompli* in staffing, or in training, and expect him to live with it. On most things Hunter allowed Wickham free rein, but he was always concerned to ensure that the Mission, though necessarily on the frontier, remained integrated with conventional, Church-based, Christian life.

The experience of SIM led to a development of Hunter's thinking about industrial mission. In the 1940s he had laid most emphasis on the class nature of the divide: middle-class Christians set over against the industrial working class. By the 1950s his analysis stressed secularisation as the greatest and most dangerous element of the division: the spiritually alive Christian standing over against the secular, amoral worker. To close the gulf he worked towards both the revitalisation of the Churches, and direct contact with the industrial working class. Industrial mission was to be one claw of a pincer movement.

Training was a practical and a symbolic sphere in which these twin objectives came together. Training the laity and the clergy at all levels was close to Hunter's heart, and he committed a great deal of his episcopal energies to developing new and more appropriate methods.

In 1950 SIM organised a summer conference for ordinands. Wickham and Hunter had spoken at a number of theological training colleges through 1949. 15 or 20 applicants were expected: 50 wrote in and some had to be placed on a waiting list. In 1951 there were 40 ordinands and some theological college staff. Summer conferences were an introduction to industrial mission rather than an attempt to train ordinands in a few days. They were a fertile source of future recruits to industrial mission in Sheffield and elsewhere: Michael Jackson, Philip Bloy and Bill Wright were all at the first conference. Simon Phipps and Michael Atkinson, for example, were on subsequent conferences. There was never any shortage of recruits.

The 1949 Conference with CACTM was also to bear fruit. In 1950 a pilot scheme was agreed by which ordinands would lodge in working-class homes and work on the shop-floor as ordinary labourers with no special privileges, although they would avoid regular Sunday work. They would be supervised by a priest-director and be given academic training. Shop-floor placements were available for many people at different points in their training. By no means all were given personal supervision.

Placements were arranged on a personal basis and never involved more than a few people at any one time. In 1950/51 Michael Jackson was at Firth

Vickers Stainless, and Philip Bloy (who had arranged his own employment) was at Hadfields. In 1953 there were nine ordinands employed by different works in Sheffield. These placements could be gruelling. They were designed to enable middle-class ordinands cross the class divide and absorb the realities of life on the shop floor. They showed up the inadequacy of previous experience, training and spirituality. One person reported that he had torn up his Franciscan homilies as a consequence; others felt that their ministries were affected for the rest of their lives by the experience. Some, including Bill Dudman and Peter Challen, remained in industrial mission work for most of their subsequent ministry.

There were never enough hours in the day. Work expanded as fast as there were chaplains available, and firms were often kept waiting for some time. Wickham found himself increasingly involved in company training programmes, beginning in Firth Brown and Samuel Fox's in 1952. There were more meetings outside the works, and a regular programme of conferences was instigated from 1951.

Works visiting remained the foundation of the Mission. Steel Peech and Tozer was the major steel producer in Rotherham. The growth of the Mission's activity in the company was only exceptional in that it had been the first firm Bishop Hunter had been able to visit and talk to people on the shop floor. Earlier attempts to visit steel works had been rebuffed. In January 1944 he had tested out the idea of a works padre with some of the shop-floor workers, and that April he introduced Wickham to them as his industrial chaplain. Wickham kept intermittent contact with the company. In 1946 a manager in the Ickles machine shop started an industrial mission group on his own initiative, but this did not last long. From 1952, the firm sent 18 people or so each year to the Mission's conferences, and by 1959 around 100 people had attended. In 1954 Scott Paradise was appointed as chaplain to the company and meetings proliferated. Four years later an estimated 500-600 workers were directly involved in around 50 separate meetings, and there were more people on the fringes. By 1959 there were 20 lay leaders in the company, enough to justify a residential conference for them alone. In this company SIM enjoyed widespread support from shop-floor and management alike.

Hunter appointed Kay Hancock in January 1953 to work with women in industry. To get the feel of Sheffield's industry she began work on the shop floor of Richards Brothers, cutlery makers, as an employee. In her first fortnight she earned £2/12/4, commenting that it was a "nice pick up". She also had to go to hospital, having damaged her hand in a particularly dangerous machine. She was not supposed to reveal why she was there, but this soon came out as the other women asked her about herself. Besides her employment she was also to go to dances, to take part in sports, netball, and generally to "muck in". This was an introduction to the industrial and social context of the Mission through "wasting time purposefully", or "loitering with intent": the experiential process of imbibing working-class life and culture, almost by osmosis. Hancock was a qualified Moral Welfare worker, and after nine months Hunter abruptly removed her from Richards Brothers and asked her to take over the Diocesan Moral Welfare work after the previous post holder died suddenly.

After a few months Hancock returned to the Mission. She visited a number of firms including Spear and Jackson and Balfour-Darwin's. In addition she extended industrial mission to two food manufacturing plants, Batchelors and Bassetts, which employed large numbers of women workers. But her main area of work was with young people. She built up a large network of young people from across Sheffield who would meet at Church House on a Sunday evening. Much of the activity was social, but the meeting's cornerstone was a regular programme of speakers tackling a range of subjects chosen by the group. As with adults there was a great deal of interest in an open and energetic Christianity, and a great deal of ignorance about the Churches and prejudice against them. Hancock took groups of young people preparing for confirmation. This led to a problem. Hunter would only confirm them to a parish Church, but few parish Churches had the vitality or the acceptance of young people that SIM could offer. Those attracted to Christianity because of the Mission would not step easily into the Churches.

All works visiting, and all the Mission's other activities, were directed to the aim of building up a body of Christians in the works. Where someone showed an initial interest, they were encouraged to become more involved, perhaps by convening a group around them in their works. They would be drawn at their own pace further into the thinking and work of the Mission. A great many of the people who supported the Mission would not have described themselves as Christians. But as they became more involved the question of their personal commitment to the Christian faith was raised: would they "cross the line" to become a Christian? The test of commitment was not greater involvement in the Mission's activities, but whether the individual felt able to worship with others, and in particular to receive Holy Communion.

Many of the most committed lay members of the Mission attended the Sunday evening Faith and Fellowship Movement. During the winter of 1949/50 they again reviewed their progress. They acknowledged that they were not attracting the working class, and they were in danger of becoming a separate clique. Accordingly they determined to stop the Sunday group altogether, and at the same time to reform the Thursday group. The Thursday gathering became the meeting place for committed lay people. On the other hand they also encouraged members to leave the group to set up further mission groups at work, or at home, or based on existing friendships.

After considerable discussion a document was agreed which was put to all members of the Thursday and Sunday groups in April 1950. It summarised the stage they had reached, and challenged others to go forward with them.

TO ALL FRIENDS OF THE INDUSTRIAL MISSION IN THE DIOCESE OF SHEFFIELD

A note on Why and How we should make a Step Forward and Grow into the Church

In the last few years the Industrial Mission has made a vast number of contacts. We can now say that given persistence, conviction about the work, and cooperation, we have really learned how to meet men in industry. If nothing else we can claim that this has been demonstrated to thousands of men and women in the works situation, that the Church does care about them; and is concerned to meet them, learn from them and share with them the faith that is committed to the Christian Church. This is a lot to claim, but it is not enough.

It is not enough to break down barriers, establish good will, and win a certain amount of respect for Christian. It is good, but not enough. To illustrate what we mean – take for example the great movement like the Trade Unions. It would never have been enough to tell men how valuable the principles of unionism were, or for organising secretaries to address men. The men had to be organised --- they had to build up an organisation. *They had to join the Movement.*

So with Christianity. Its strength is never realised until men *join the movement*, throw in their lot with it, and are themselves helped by it as they themselves help it forward. *The Movement Christians join is the Christian Church.*

It is a movement you join for life and it is open to all who profess faith in God.

The instrument of the Church in the industrial field is the Industrial Mission.

The Church, if you like, is God's union. It is not an alternative to other movements, but a place where men derive strength, insight, forgiveness and the new outlook that they need to take into every other society that they belong to – home, work, union, political party, club, sport, and so on.

Theoretically this is simple, you belong to God's union by belonging to the local Church or Chapel in your area, but as you know in practice it doesn't work like this. Again, rather like the Trade Unions, you are supposed to go to the local branch, but unfortunately except for the few it just doesn't happen. That is why we have the Industrial Mission, which is the movement of the Church into the situation of industry. By making this step in the Industrial Mission you belong to the Church. Those who come fully into this venture, and make this step together, are sharing a full expression of the Christian Church – even if they never go anywhere on Sunday. This is not to rule out Sunday worship, of course, but it is to explain that by our own actions in this way we are *being the Church in the fullest sense.*

What the Step Forward entails

It means *coming over the line* as committed Christians.

That is becoming members of the Corporate Christian Church. As such and as a mission to industry, we are obliged to do the following:

1. **Worship God Together** – which is the way we show our faith in God together and derive strength from God together. (Just as a plant grows in strength and stature by facing the sun and the light.) The Christian Church, in all its branches, has done this since the time of Christ. It has done it by learning from God's word, and by receiving the bread and wine at the Lord's Supper, the Holy Communion. (NB. We may not understand much of this yet, that is understandable and means that we have some study to do.)

2. **Study Together** – All kinds of things: Christianity itself, the world we live in, its problems and difficulties (including home life, politics, social problems) and we need to study these from a Christian point of view.

3. **Plan Together** – (for an effective mission to industry): What we ought to do, what we can do, how we can help, problems of our members, how we can advance and involve others, what special project we ought to run, bearing one another's burdens etc.

4. **Have Fellowship Together** – this grows naturally and deeply when we do the above, so comradeship grows by lifting us out of our little ruts in the sense of a common cause in the world.

The task of the Industrial Mission then is, from our industrial contacts to build up the Christian Church with all these marks. If we can do this it means that at the heart and centre of all our contact work there is steadily being built up a *core of militants – of active workers –* which is both the foundation of this work and also its spearhead. Something you can build up and something that thrusts forward into all kinds of ventures. We should both be the Church in all its fullness and at the same time be an instrument to do mission work of the Church in an industrial society.

It is an expression of the Church equipped for a new kind of job that we ask you to join. We are willing to build slowly but we must build surely. We must not take this step unless we are really sure about it.

You may ask – Why do we do this? Why do we make this Industrial Mission of the Church?

The answer is simple – because we believe that Christianity is God's truth for all mankind, that the healing of this world is bound up with men believing and living as Christians, and that the purpose of life is discovered in our obedience to God.

If you accept this, if you think this is right – *will you come in with us?*[11]

Those who accepted this challenge continued to meet on Thursdays. It was noticeable that a number of communists who had attended the old, open discussion group could not accede to the new regimen. The new Thursday Evening Group comprised the most committed lay leaders of the movement.

From 1951, following the reorientation of the Thursday Evening Group, new discussion groups began to develop outside working hours from 1951, though many were short lived.[12] Most were groups of people from a single department or works where meetings were impractical, or who wanted more time for debate, and who decided to meet away from their office or shop floor. Other meetings drew members from a mixture of companies. In 1954 Philip Bloy began a managers' group aimed at the younger managers who lived near him in the Millhouses area of Sheffield. Some groups developed study programmes and kept careful minutes. Others remained more informal.

Leaders of these groups, and leaders who convened and led groups in the works, were invited to the Thursday Evening Group which thus became a loose form of staff meeting, enabling lay leaders in the different parts in Sheffield to keep in touch with one another. It comprised the central meeting of the mission and it set the pace for the development of lay leadership.

Once a month the Thursday Evening Group began with Holy Communion. It was open to all, lay leader or not, Anglican or not, and was extended to those who had "crossed the line" even if they were not confirmed. They avoided the Book of Common Prayer and used a form of service tailored to the Group. Certain actions were stressed in ways that prefigured the more communal ethos of the Alternative Service Book, 1980. The handshake of peace was given as an act of reconciliation for the whole Church. Communicants gathered around the Lord's Table and Christian names were used in the administration.

In 1953/54 a small group was asked to look at the place of worship in the mission. They reported that Holy Communion was a rock, a stable point from which a true perspective on the secular world was possible. In worship, they said, the believer stands in the right place from which to look out

"at our work in the city and steel-works of Sheffield. We have not tried to stand the Lord's Supper on its head to suit the supposed needs of our work. In our work we have to be the sort of men who take part in the Lord's Supper. This means that the mysterious action of the Lord's Supper has to be left to speak for itself. We have to grow into it, not adapt it to ourselves. Thus we become the recommendation for it."[13]

To join in worship was a visible expression of "crossing the line". It was thus also the test of the Mission as a whole: if ordinary working men and women did not grow into worship then the gulf between Christianity and the workers had not been bridged.

In this statement the report also voiced what the Mission perceived to be the right relationship between Christianity and the secular world. To see issues from a Christian perspective was to see them from a deeper reality. New techniques and new language might be needed for the Mission to be effective, but there was no question about the absolute and unchangeable nature of the faith itself. People committed themselves to the Christian faith; the faith was not amended to suit them.

A further development in the early 1950s was the rapid growth of residential conferences. In 1951 three people had attended a successful conference in Manchester organised by the William Temple Foundation on "The Moral Problems of our Industrial Society". Wickham proposed a similar conference in Sheffield aimed at training lay leaders. The Bishop's Advisory Committee considered the proposal and thought that a long weekend would be the right length of time, but they were worried about the financial implications. Twenty-four people from six firms attended the first "Christian Leadership in Industry" conference at William Temple College, Hawarden, in September 1951. It had immediate results: in Edgar Allens a lay leaders committee was formed; a further conference was proposed for Samuel Fox's lay leaders; Steel Peech and Tozer had initiated some industrial mission activity; and it had led to further openings for the Mission in a number of firms. A second conference was held in January 1952. Subsequently Hunter called a number of industrialists together who assured him that they would support these conferences, and that they foresaw no financial problems. Hunter and Wickham worked well together.

Conferences rapidly became a significant part of the Mission's activities. They developed into different types. The most frequent were "inter-works" conferences, held three or four times a year. Invitations would be sent to firms, including those with no regular chaplaincy, asking them to send a number of managers and shop-floor workers to the conferences. Deliberate attempts were made to include people active in the trades unions or on works councils. Around 25 men, and the occasional woman, would come together from up to 20 works, almost all on paid leave of absence. Other conferences drew their members from a single works. Many of those attending had no contact with Christianity, outside weddings, funerals, and prejudice, but they often returned to their firms enthusing about the value of industrial mission.

Each conference followed the same basic pattern, though without uniformity. They were three-day gatherings beginning on a Thursday evening and ending on the Sunday afternoon, frequently held at the diocesan conference centre, Whirlow Grange. Each one began with dinner, and a tone of warmth and welcome was established which would encourage open, enthusiastic, often humorous discussion. On the Friday a senior manager or trades unionist would introduce an industrial topic. Saturday began with a speaker exploring the meaning of modern Christianity. Time was put aside for discussion, and panels of experts would be organised to field questions. The conference ended with a description of the work of SIM, and discussion of ways in which it could be further promoted in the works.

There was no soft sell about industrial mission. Chaplains preached the Gospel explicitly and energetically. They dismissed a Christianity which comprised unthinking belief in certain dogmas, or merely demanded attendance at Church and confirmation. The faith they proclaimed was that all were called to be fellow workers with God in furthering His purposes for humanity.

The kernel of SIM's spirituality was encapsulated in one of Wickham's metaphors. The Churches were, he said, fishing in muddy waters. They thought that their task was to pull people out and to place them in the clean waters of the Church. By contrast, the task of industrial mission was to clean up the water. If SIM ever drew people out, it was simply to return them better able to help clean up the pool.

The world was God's world and was essentially good. The revelation of God in Jesus Christ meant that communion between God and his creatures was possible. Jesus came to enable a deaf world to hear and a blind world to see. The task of faith was first to perceive the world as it truly was. Everyone needed, in Wickham's words, "to put on the spectacles of faith".

Christian discipleship was all-embracing.

> "In addition to doing a good job of work, we have to make decisions and judgements, adopt attitudes, frame policies, examine motives, and analyse situations, in the light of the Christian beliefs about God and man, and the true purpose of life, society, and history."[14]

Faith was both personal and structural. To work with God was to become fully human. Industry was valuable, but in itself it was a morally neutral tool to be directed to good or evil. The Christian goal for industry, and for other aspects of modern life, was that it should function in ways that would further

God's Providence. The task of the Christian in industry was to work in accordance with God's dynamic plan, and to contribute to this aim in all that they did. If the Mission was successful then industry itself would be imbued, or stained, with Christian values. The implication of success was immeasurable. Industry was the lever which could move society, therefore if industry lived by Christian values then it followed that the whole secular order would be rechristianised.

This was the clean water: a society which was just, fair and caring; a world where people went the second mile, going beyond duty in service to others. Great emphasis was placed on encouraging thoughtful and reflective leadership in society, whether Christian or not. Industry was to serve society. Christians were to take responsibility for others. Justice was central. One person remembered the Biblical injunction to honesty, "you shall not make the ephah small nor the shekel great";[15] another recalled the phrase, "a fair day's work for a fair day's pay".[16] Despite a general affirmation of industry, there was a recognition that bad practices were rife. Justice required action by all sides of industry.

In asserting the need for justice, and in encouraging political and industrial leadership against the background of the cold war, SIM trod a precarious political path. The Mission was always viewed with suspicion by some on both sides of industry. One retired manager recalled Wickham as having a Bible in one hand and Marx in the other, and in the early 1950s the anti-communist Moral Re-armament organisation had tried to taint him as a Russian fellow-traveller. Hunter, however, saw the Mission and the christianising of industry in part as a bulwark against communism, a view not generally shared by the chaplains.

As a Church organisation SIM consciously steered clear of partisan allegiance in both industrial and civic politics. Yet chaplains were on the whole left of centre in their personal political views, though not all were Labour party supporters. Wickham later acknowledged considerable debt to Marx and Marxist categories, though to have done so openly at the time would have prejudiced his work in industry.[17]

It would be wrong to give the impression that the task of the chaplains was simply to convey a fixed corpus of Christian thought. There were fundamental and objective truths of Christianity which could be brought to bear on industry, though neither SIM, nor Christian belief, nor the Bible could offer detailed answers or a blueprint for the complexities of modern industrial life.

Two principles guided the application of Christianity to the secular world. These were "middle axioms" and "the autonomy of the secular".

"Middle axioms" were second order concepts derived from the overarching truths of Christianity. For example, the Christian truth that all human beings were fallen creatures gave rise to the middle axiom that no-one was infallible. "Middle axioms" could thus attract assent from people who would not call themselves Christians. They provided broad guidelines for moral action but were still at a level of generality which left individuals to work out the details for themselves. Nor would, or should, clergy involve themselves in the substance of social or industrial dilemmas. "The autonomy of the secular" implied that decisions in the secular realm should be left to secular experts. Clergy had no particular expertise to contribute, and there were no specifically Christian answers. Chaplains could encourage and support people facing difficult decisions, and they could offer advice from the sidelines on taking those decisions morally, but they were essentially observers, not players in the industrial game.

Thus faith was the process of becoming Christian, discipleship was working things out in practice; "crossing the line" was a stage on the journey, not a statement of arrival. Chaplains argued and wrestled with the workers in the most down-to-earth terms and in sophisticated theological debate. Through Wickham the Mission was engrossed in some of the most up-to-date theological questioning. Factory workers wrote to Rudolf Bultmann on questions of "demythologising" at a time when such debates were hardly known outside learned journals. At every level in the works people responded positively to Wickham and his message; a few wanted to go ever deeper into the Christian faith.

1955-1959, The Church outside the Church

In 1955 a Second Line conference was held at William Temple College, Rugby. The front line comprised lay people who, by their lives and activities, were undertaking the mission in the works. The second line was the back-up which would nurture, train, encourage, and support lay missionaries at the front line. This was a significant step forward.

"Canon Wickham opened the Conference by reminding us that the Industrial Mission was at a new stage in its development, a stage where lay people were beginning to play a more active and important part, and that the lay people that were present were actually representing a piece of work – a project if you like – that was now being performed, and that this conference was a means of such people coming together to think more deeply and to share their thoughts with each other, whereby the projects for which they were responsible could be strengthened and sustained."[18]

After 10 years gestation the "lay project" was born. Christian lay leaders in the works would henceforth take much greater responsibility for steering the Mission towards its destination. They were a vital step towards what was variously described as the "para-church", the "Church outside the Church", or the "Church without walls". Lay projects were a "new expression of the Church" appropriate to industrial society. They were new, small, and fragile, but definitely alive and kicking.

Lay projects were much more significant than the snap-break meeting. Snap-break meetings were vehicles by which chaplains could engage the workers. The job of their lay leaders was to gather people together for the meetings; to sustain interest between chaplains' visits; to develop their own Christian discipleship with others in the same works or department; and on occasions to offer pastoral care, or to refer those in need of such support to the chaplains. Lay projects, however, belonged wholly to the workers. Chaplains might encourage their formation, and keep close contact with them, but each group was autonomous and would be allowed to grow and to die in its own time.

Lay projects were supported through two structures. In the main companies a lay Industrial Mission committee was established to oversee the development of the Mission and to co-ordinate groups in networks which mirrored the structure of the company. In Samuel Fox, for example, there was at one point a lay leader in each of the works' departments.

Secondly, groups kept in touch through the central Lay Leaders' meetings in Sheffield. After the 1955 conference a new Saturday Evening meeting of lay leaders was formed from the Thursday Evening Group membership. This met most months at Church House under the leadership of Ted Wickham. Lay leaders would report on progress in their group, and this would be followed by training in Bible study, theology, or the crafts of building and running groups. All lay leaders were invited to these meetings. Once a quarter they would hold an open meeting, often with a speaker; each June the open meeting was SIM's Annual General Meeting. Lay leaders were, and saw themselves as, the apex of the development of a new expression of the Church in industry.

Margaret Kane described one wet Saturday in the autumn of 1959:

"There were about thirty of us present and the room seemed packed to capacity, as piles of raincoats on the tables grew higher,

Scott Paradise with furnace bricklayers; Steel, Peech and Tozer, 1956.

Steelworkers' Conference at William Temple College, Rugby. Ted Wickham, front row left.

Michael Jackson with railway workers at Darnall Locomotive sheds, 1959.

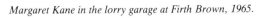

Margaret Kane in the lorry garage at Firth Brown, 1965.

and the group around the fire continually opened up to squeeze late-comers in. Manual workers can often be distinguished by their build. Alf, with his shock of greying hair and rough outbursts of comment was an outsize man in every way, and Sam, another roller, was over six feet tall. Between them George and Henry looked slight and wiry. Several of those present were clerical workers and there were a few managers, not yet of much seniority. The leader of the Mission chaired the meeting, sitting well back in his chair in easy relaxation.

"All the subjects were introduced by laymen. First came reports – Bernard, a clerical worker, described a new venture in which a group of people who lived and worked in the same district were studying 'The Problem of Youth at Stocksbridge'. From the other extreme of Industrial Mission's spread, George reported on a conference held for twenty Industrial Mission supporters from his own firm. Then David, a young man with a keen political concern, gave a report of work being done by a small group on 'Social Problems of the Recession'.

"The second half of the evening consisted of Bible Study. The Chairman reminded people of the syllabus we were following on 'The Parables of the Kingdom', and Geoff, a small man with heavy lines on his face, introduced the parable for the evening – the Strong Man Bound (Matthew 12:29-30). Discussion was lively and, apart from the Chairman's firm underlining of the important points, the other chaplains tried to forget their professional training and listened to the laymen as they approached the Bible with freshness and simplicity."[19]

The structures by which lay projects could be developed and sustained, though essential, were transient and secondary. What was of primary importance was that men and women could meet Christianity face to face in their own work place. There the Christian faith was expounded by people of their own social class. There was no space for hypocrisy or pious preaching, only for living out the Gospel. The spirituality of the Mission, its chaplains and its lay leaders, was tested and proved in the furnaces of Sheffield's steel works. Wickham described the lay projects as "the most audacious and creative mission experiments in recent years".[20]

The strength of lay leadership could be counted in the numbers attending the monthly service of Holy Communion, moved in 1955 from Church House to the Cathedral at Hunter's insistence. From 1955 to July 1958 about 20-30 people attended Holy Communion, and numbers showed a slight growth through this period. Between July 1958 and July 1960 numbers were higher, varying between 30 and 50.

Yet, perhaps because joining in worship was a visible expression of commitment, of "crossing the line", Holy Communion was also curiously divisive. Some lay leaders would not participate, but would wait outside for the meeting proper to begin. Some felt their unwillingness to worship to be a personal failure, or that they lacked some spiritual grace. Although there were exceptions, those who participated in worship were by and large lay leaders drawn from office staff and management while those who hung back were from the shop floor. Not even the Mission could overcome the reality of class and industrial stratification.

The development of the lay projects was not yet strong enough to challenge SIM's existing superstructure. The Bishops' Advisory Committee continued to have oversight of the Mission's development. However in 1957, at the lay leaders request, a finance sub-committee was set up with membership drawn equally from the Advisory Committee and the Saturday Lay Leaders meeting. Industry continued to provide around two thirds of the Mission's regular income. Employee giving schemes were extended to Firth Vickers Stainless (from 1956) and Jessop Saville (from 1958). Other firms made lump sum donations and gave assistance in kind. Hadfields, for example, provided its chaplain, Philip Bloy, with a car at one point. Most companies provided their chaplains with secretarial facilities. Expenses rose as new chaplains were appointed – by the end of 1959 there were eight full-time chaplains.

There were other organisational changes. In the second half of the 1950s Wickham spent little time on the shop floor, and more on the development of the ideas of Industrial Mission. In 1955 he was appointed Stephenson Fellow at the University of Sheffield in order to write his first book, though he continued to direct SIM. For part of 1957 he went to the United States on a lecture tour, meeting many of the senior theologians on whom he and Industrial Mission had drawn, including Richard and Reinhold Neibuhr and Paul Tillich. In 1958 he was seconded for one third of his time to be Secretary of the Social and Industrial Council of the Church Assembly.

Training continued to be an important focus of the Mission's activities. Until the mid-1950s the majority of ordinands had completed National Service and came to Sheffield with some experience of life. From 1957 National Service was wound down, and in 1959 it was abolished. Two theological colleges, Kelham and King's College, London, agreed to send ordinands on a regular basis before they began their training. John Rogan was given oversight of these students. These were 18-year-old school leavers, and Hunter later commented that they had not had the spiritual and theological depth to make the most of the placement.[21]

In another scheme Roland Walls, then at Cambridge University, agreed in 1958 to supervise a project in which a small group of older, graduate ordinands would spend six months in industry, and a further six months sharing a house with him as tutor and supervisor. They would follow a course of guided reading, study, including Greek, and spiritual reflection. This was less to Wickham's taste as Walls was concerned to develop a devotional spirituality which did not cohere with Wickham's ethos of mission. Walls left in 1960 and John Rogan added this scheme to his responsibilities.

Things did not always run smoothly. One trainee marched up to the management in his first week to complain that the canteen facilities were not clean enough. Another, on a day trip to Blackpool, spent his time visiting every Anglican church he could find. And on one occasion a landlady demanded that Wickham remove the student lodging with her. He was coming home exhausted, covered in steel-works dust, and he didn't even take off his boots before collapsing on the bed! However between 1950 and 1966 over 200 ordinands had experience of this mixture of shop-floor and theological training in Sheffield, in addition to those visiting on the summer courses.

In the works the daily routine kept chaplains busy. The week began at 7.30am on Monday morning with Holy Communion, corporate contemplation, and a staff meeting which would finish around 1pm. The meeting would pick a topic for discussion and that would then be raised thematically in the daily round of visiting and snap-break meetings.

The "Sheffield model" remained the foundation of the work though it was developed and refined. More missioners meant that more than one could visit the same company. One would be assigned the lead role, visiting perhaps three days a week, and another would take a secondary role, perhaps visiting one day a week. The roles were known in the team as "King" and "Crown Prince" respectively (this did not reflect seniority, roles were interchangeable in different works). Snap-break meetings had to be regular, but not too frequent, open and public, and chaplains often worked on a six-week timetable of visits. Chaplains would try to arrive early and stay late to be able to talk around the meeting. Pastoral work, including home and hospital visits, was frequent, though always as a consequence and not as an aim of works visiting. Continuity of visiting was important: SIM was engaged in a sustained long-term enterprise. Wickham was scathing about the dilettantism of so much of the Church's approach to industry. At the same time other activities were added to the basic model. Educational work with apprentices began to take up a significant amount of time, as did the development of systematic links with professional organisations and trades unions.

John Rogan recalled the programme of a day when he would visit Samuel Fox:

8.00am	Arrive at Samuel Fox
8.30	meeting
9.00	shop floor visiting
11.00	lecture apprentices at the nearby College of Further Education
12.30	shop floor meeting
1.30pm	white collar meeting, or lunch with management
Afternoon	visiting around the works
5.30pm	shift break meeting

The day might finish after the 5.30pm meeting, or it might go on with further visiting, or an evening meeting. There were also home and hospital visits to be arranged and, for Rogan, responsibilities to students on placement. Life was not all serious and the team often socialised together.

In Hadfields Philip Bloy began the work in 1952 and continued until 1959. He began in the foundry and the No. 1 machine shop, and gradually extended visiting until he covered all parts of the works. Some places had shop floor meetings, but in much of the firm the pattern of work or the level of noise made this inappropriate. He held regular discussion groups outside office hours for shop-floor workers, apprentices, office staff, and management. An "over-21s" group was started in 1958. Around 50 adults and 40 apprentices had attended the Mission's conferences by 1960. Good Friday and Christmas Carol services were held.

Meetings continued to play a major part in the work of the mission. Mr Norman Jenkinson, a lay leader of long standing in Steel Peech and Tozer, reported on the Bar Mill group which met after work in the Bridge Inn, Rotherham, as they had only 20 minutes for lunch,

> "The meeting consisted of Communists, Church of England, atheists and agnostics. There were those who went to church regularly and those who only went when they were carried there.
> "The aims of the group were to foster better relations between the men, between the shifts, and between management and men. An effort was made to get the men talking about serious subjects and broaden their outlook on life."

Topics included: the hydrogen bomb; whether the teaching of the Bible could be related to modern life; whether the Church had failed, and if so, why; what kind of Church did people want; and spiritual healing. Jenkinson added,

> "To his knowledge, quite a lot of men had been surprised and impressed by the help and advice given by the padre at times of difficulty. He was quite sure that there was a greater spirit of tolerance and wellbeing amongst the men on the Works than ever before."[22]

Another type of evening meeting was the "Frontier Group", first started in Rotherham in 1955. This was an attempt to provide a forum for lay people who felt themselves to be most concerned to work out the relationship of the Christian faith to the secular world, and in particular the political world. It drew people together from a number of worksites in the Rotherham area. A Stocksbridge Frontier Group had a membership restricted to those who both worked in Fox's, and lived in the Stocksbridge area. They established a study programme looking at current problems in the area. The Sheffield Frontier Group began in 1959. It became a route by which the chaplains might engage with full time trades union officials, city councillors, and other with civic responsibilities. Because of its range of contacts in industry, and especially, in a Labour dominated political context, its access to and support from the trades unions, SIM was perceived to be an increasingly influential body in local affairs.[23]

SIM continued to extend and develop its visiting base and in 1958 it began work in British Rail. Independently of SIM Gerald Hollis had visited the Railway Plant works in Doncaster with Hunter's encouragement since 1952. His work had impressed Sir Brian Robertson, Chairman of the British

Transport Commission, who discussed with Bishop Hunter the possibility of extending the work to other areas, especially Derby, Crewe, and Swindon. In 1957 Hunter wrote to the Bishops of these areas, and Robertson approached the railway's Regional Boards. In Sheffield the Divisional Manager who was also a committed Christian then contacted SIM.

A year of negotiations with the unions followed before chaplaincy work could begin. The structure of the railways implied a modification of the pattern of chaplaincy which had evolved in the steel works. Chaplains concentrated on the larger depots and built up a network of lay groups which came together in a six-monthly general meeting. Support from management was consistent, but relations with the different unions varied considerably, largely depending on the personal contact chaplains had with union leaders in each depot. Success showed SIM that their basic approach was not confined to steel production and engineering works. With suitable adaptation the "Sheffield model" could be applied to other industries.

SIM was by no means always successful. Some managements distrusted the Mission. On rare occasions chaplains were asked not to return, usually for being too enthusiastic in encouraging union activity and thus breaking the implicit contract with management. In Balfour's (later Balfour-Darwin's) Wickham had held meetings in an engineering tool works in the 1940s. In the management's eyes SIM was thereafter tainted with that department's left-wing reputation, a view reinforced in the early 1960s when Margaret Kane was partially instrumental in establishing a branch of the British Iron, Steel and Kindred Trades Association (BISAKTA) in another of the firm's works.

If work in industry was going well, relations with the parishes and local churches continued to be divided. SIM had considerable support from a minority of parish clergy, and vocal opposition from others. The chaplains' daily experience was grounded in the works, and increasingly they looked at the Church with the eyes of outsiders. The gulf they perceived was the distance between spiritually dead churches, concerned only to perpetuate themselves, and the urgent, dynamic and vital demands of the gospel given substance in the works.

The contrast was pervasive. Churches had static or falling congregations; the missioners' presentation of the Christian message met with an enthusiastic response from many of the people least likely to set foot in a Church. Congregations were introspective, conventional, middle-class and dull; Industrial Mission proclaimed the excitement of the liberating power of the Gospel. Church-going Christians received little or no support in relation to the personal and ethical ambiguities of modern working life; industrial chaplains were constantly exploring these issues. Chaplains held the Church wholly responsible for the gulf, and some of them, notably Wickham, could be uncharitable in this message. They said that God was *not* calling people to go into the Churches as they were at present. One person remembered Wickham in an informal meeting warning apprentices against parish clergy: all they wanted to do, he said, was to trap people in a Church box, and snap shut the lid. Not surprisingly, some parish clergy resented the Mission.

Nevertheless considerable energy was put into strengthening the link between the Mission and the parishes, and other parish clergy gave the Mission consistent support. All missioners were attached to local churches. They preached, took services, attended Church Councils and Chapter meetings. They provided cover for holidays and sickness. Relationships with their parish clergy varied, but were generally positive. A significant minority of lay leaders in the works were also members of local congregations, by no means solely Anglican. A few clergy, especially outside Sheffield itself, undertook some works visiting along the Mission's lines as part of their parochial responsibilities.

Wickham was forthright in his attack on the Church's self-delusion. The parochial sophistry of the Church of England was that every blade of grass in England lay within a parish, and that therefore the Church was all-encompassing. Wickham showed in his book *Church and People in an Industrial City*, published in 1957, that the Church had not lost the industrial working classes, it had never contained them. His detailed evidence showed that the Church's claim to be all-encompassing was a self-serving deceit glossing over the patently sectional, middle-class nature of the Church. Worse still, the inexorable haemorrhage of church-goers and the progressive debilitation of the Church's power and influence implied only one prognosis: the Church of England was dying.[24]

Yet it need not! The welcome given to the Gospel by ordinary working men and women, and the enthusiastic response of some, proved that the right approach could reap rich rewards. If the Church took Wickham's medicine it could yet recover and attain its rightful place as a great, comprehensive, national Church.[25] The medicine Wickham prescribed was a theological revolution, the end of the parochial structure and the creation of a new organisation, and a new relationship with the secular world.[26] However, if the Church refused the medicine it would assuredly die. And in those circumstances Christian members of the industrial para-church would emerge from the works like survivors of an earthquake emerging from the rubble. Lay groups were both the vanguard of the new expression of the Church, and also guarantors of the Gospel itself.

The reformation of the Church was a long-term goal. The immediate task for Wickham was to establish his control over the burgeoning industrial mission movement. Through the 1950s there was some industrial work in most dioceses of the Church of England. The great bulk of industrial visiting was undertaken by parish clergy as part of their pastoral role, but more specialist full-time appointments were being made. A growing number of Methodist ministers, thanks in large part to the Luton Industrial College, also undertook works visiting, at times in isolation from the Anglicans. Individuals and projects in other denominations were also involved in work with industry.

Sheffield Industrial Mission was highly influential in the national development of industrial mission. SIM offered extensive on-the-job training as chaplains for other dioceses. Bill Wright founded the Teeside Industrial Mission. He deferred ordination in order to gain practical experience in industry in Sunderland. Michael Ramsey, then Bishop of Durham, ordained him and sent him to Sheffield where he stayed for four years working as a member of the team. On his return he was appointed as the Bishop's industrial advisor and industrial chaplain. Scott Paradise had come for three years training from Detroit, Michigan. Sheffield chaplains were also exported to set up other industrial missions. In 1957 Michael Brooke went to Manchester and in 1959 Philip Bloy was seconded to Nigeria for three months. The continual flow of ordinands on placements in industry or attending the summer courses spread knowledge of industrial mission and the ideas on which it was built.

SIM's acknowledged preeminence also drew to it a continual stream of visitors from many other countries, including Canada, Australia, and Japan. Many of the visitors came to learn from Sheffield's experience in order to assist the establishment of industrial mission in their own country. Hunter and Wickham spoke about the Mission in Britain, in Europe, and in America. Hunter was well respected and well connected in church circles throughout Europe and the United Kingdom, and he had strong links with the World Council of Churches. He contributed, amongst many other gatherings, to the Lambeth Conferences of both 1948 and 1958. Wickham was similarly well connected, especially in those parts of the WCC concerned with urban and industrial mission. He also had opportunities to reach a wider audience through television and radio broadcasts.

But influence was not control. Bill Gowland, who founded and ran the Luton Industrial College, remained fiercely independent and critical of Wickham's theology. Colin Cuttell in London, Cuthbert Bardsley's successor, was strongly opposed to Wickham's approach. He wrote,

"It is a pity that the tag 'industrial chaplain' was ever invented. It raises doubts and resentments, suggesting short cuts to the Kingdom-of-God-on-earth by way of a special brand of religion aimed at a new collective called the 'industrial proletariat'."[27]

There was little love lost here. Others developed work on different lines, John Ragg in Bristol, for example, and Ralph Stevens in Birmingham. The very growth and diversification of industrial mission had encouraged the spread of alternative models and other understandings of the purpose and function of mission in industry. Wickham's drive to promote industrial mission was also a drive to promote his particular vision.

One other influence threatened Wickham's vision, not by dilution but by its strength. The worker-priest movement, despite its troubles continued to inspire some in Britain, especially in the first half of the 1950s. There was a handful of Anglican worker-priests in the 1950s.[28] They were critical of industrial mission. They argued that because chaplains only visited factories with management's blessing, they were therefore management's tools. Furthermore, industrial mission was based on three false assumptions: that workers have a religious need which can be satisfied by chaplains' consultations; that priests assume that they have something to give their hearers and are able to re-animate the religious spirit rather than quench it; and finally that the lack of explicit protest against religious activities means that the workers accept it. In fact workers were likely to respond equally positively to any break in the routine.

Wickham fought back. He argued that the missionary task was different in England from the circumstances of France. British workers were neither so secularised, nor so anti-clerical as their French equivalents. Second, worker-priests established little, factional cells which were in effect separate congregations and were not furthering the development of the national Church. Third, and crucially, Wickham's vision was one in which the laity were central. He never set out to build an organisation of visiting priests, and he was convinced that working priests would further constrain the witness of the laity.

By the mid-1950s Wickham was working hard to gain control over industrial mission nationally. His campaign had two flanks. The first pushed the British Council of Churches. In 1957 the BCC accepted the need for a co-ordinated approach to industrial mission, and set up a working party which reported in 1958. *The Church and Industry*[30] was an accomplished example of ecumenical double-speak. It acknowledged significant differences of approach, and with the tact and unquenchable optimism essential to ecumenism, opined that, with further discussion, the Holy Spirit would undoubtedly guide the Churches through their disagreements into more truth.

The second and more important flank was fought through the structures of the Church Assembly, General Synod's predecessor. Within its arcane machinery Hunter and Wickham worked in tandem. Hunter had been a friend and admirer of William Temple, but had no rapport with his successor, Archbishop Fisher. Nevertheless he was well placed to influence the workings of the Church's bureaucracy in relation to industry. He had been an active member of the Social and Industrial Council of the Church Assembly since its reconstitution in 1952. He had played a significant part in combining this body with the Moral Welfare Council to create the Board for Social Responsibility in 1958. From 1958 he was Chairman of the Industry Committee of the Board.

To be honest, Church Assembly was very little interested in industrial matters. However a trickle of debates in the mid-1950s had exposed to its members the inadequacy of the Church's links with industry. The Assembly required a report on the matter. In 1959 the Industry Committee of the Church Assembly published *The Task of the Church in Relation to Industry*.[31] The Working Party was chaired by Sir Wilfrid Garrett, previously HM Chief Inspector of Factories who had been actively aware of SIM's work for a decade; and its Secretary was Ted Wickham. Although this was a committee report its style and content bore Wickham's imprint very strongly.

The Task of the Church in Relation to Industry reviewed the range of links that the Church had with industry and, with little connecting argument, recommended a national Industrial Secretariat. This central body would develop, co-ordinate, and directly undertake industrial mission work. It would work with the Free Churches, and with the theological colleges, and would set up special training courses. It would forge links with the national headquarters of industry and trades unions, reinforcing links made locally, and reflecting the national and local structure of each industry. It would promote related study and research. In July 1959 the report was accepted by the Church Assembly along with a resolution to establish a Committee with staff, and the appropriate finance.

Wickham won the battle and lost the war.

The hierarchy of the Church of England could never accept such a powerful creation, even without Wickham's publicly avowed intention to reform the whole of the Church. The Industrial Secretariat was a cuckoo that would destroy the nest itself. Church Assembly's decision was subsequently emasculated, and Wickham was toppled from his platform.

A successful Industrial Secretariat would have removed industrial mission from the authority of diocesan bishops. Its head would have been, *de facto*, a non-territorial bishop. Furthermore the Secretariat would quickly be identified as the political agency of the Church. It would disrupt the stable, cautious connections that the Church nurtured at a national level. As a final straw, it would have been almost impossible not to appoint Wickham as head of the Secretariat. He would become the Ignatius Loyola of Industrial Mission. He was politically and ecclesiastically unacceptable.

The Church Assembly's decision was implemented, but slowly and partially. In place of a largely independent Secretariat, a sub-committee of the Board for Social Responsibility was set up. It was staffed first by John Rogan, from SIM, and by Tom Chapman, previously an official with the Amalgamated Engineering Union who had lost his post to internal communist intrigue. The committee had a concern for industrial mission, but its powers were few. It had no authority over industrial mission work on a national level, no brief to speak for the Church on industrial or political issues, and few resources.

Ted Wickham himself was neutralised as a political force. He was offered the post of Suffragan Bishop of Middleton. He had doubts about the wisdom of accepting the offer, and consulted a number of friends before deciding. The advice from Sheffield was consistent: if it would help spread the mission, take the job; if it wouldn't, don't. Bishop Hunter said,

> "He has been urged to undertake the office of a Bishop in the Church of God on the understanding that he will continue to advise and promote work in that sphere with which his name will always be associated."[32]

In fact, as a Suffragan Bishop he had little power, and less influence than he had had as Senior Industrial Chaplain in Sheffield. At the same time the impression was given to the outside world that the Church was honouring one of its most prophetic sons. Wickham would later tell friends that he had been "blackballed into the episcopacy".

As he prepared to leave Sheffield sadness at his departure was mixed with pride in his achievements. It was the visible end of a chapter in industrial mission. A special train was chartered to take the 400 people from the works who accompanied him to his consecration in York Minster on November 30th 1959. Bishop Hunter went from one end of the train to the other during the journey, and in the last carriage one man said to him, "you know, Bishop, what the Mission has done is that men can now talk freely on the shop-floor about serious subjects like religion."[33] The gulf had been bridged.

NOTES

1. "Industrial Mission", L.S. Hunter, unpublished late typescript, (undated but post-retirement)

2. The YCW was an Anglican version of the Catholic Jeunesse Ouvrière Chrétienne or "Jocists", set up by Joseph Cardijn in Belgium after the First World War. See: *The Christian Response to Industrial Capitalism,* W. Charlton, T. Mallinson, R. Oakshott, Sheed & Ward 1986, pp.203-4

3. A detailed account of first phase of the French worker-priest movement is: *The Church and Industrial Society,* Gregor Siefer, Trans. I. & F. McHugh, Dartman Longman Todd, 1964. See also: *France Pagan? The Mission of Abbé Godin,* Maisie Ward, Catholic Book Club, 1949

4. *Priest-Workman in Germany*, Henri Perrin, translated by Rosemary Sheed, Sheed and Ward, 1947; *Priest and Worker, The autobiography of Henri Perrin*, Henri Perrin, translated by Bernard Wall, The Catholic Book Club, 1964

5. Suppression was not the end of the story. The worker-priest movement was slowly re-established in France and elsewhere. In the 1950s many worker-priests had remained in their jobs in a show of passive resistance. They were not pursued, but by 1960 almost all had left the Church. Others took their place. In 1965 the Second Vatican Council recognised that manual labour could be part of a priest's life, and two years later the French Catholic Church formally reinstated worker-priests. The Cardijn Seminary was opened for their training. By 1986 there were some 1,000 worker-priests in France, about half of them in full-time factory work. See: *The Christian Response to Industrial Capitalism*, W. Charlton, T. Mallinson, R. Oakshott, Sheed and Ward, 1986.

6. The Church Burgesses are trustees of an historic local fund associated with Sheffield Cathedral, and people of established standing in Sheffield society. Mr Holstrom was SIM's Treasurer through the 1950s.

7. Interview with Mr Ken Martin

8. L.S. Hunter, *Sheffield Diocesan Review,* No. 3, March 1948; and "Industrial Mission", unpublished late typescript.

9. Master Cutler is an honorary title awarded annually to a leading member of the Cutlers' Company, an association of industrialists in Sheffield concerned with steel manufacture and metal working.

10. Kay Hancock was appointed as Kay Ellerton. She met her husband Len in Sheffield where he was working in a steel works as a student with SIM.

11. "Industrial Mission", Mr R. Hogg, unpublished manuscript, n/d [1960/61]

12. *Mission Meetings: a sketch of the work of the Sheffield Industrial Mission in the fifties and sixties,* Philip Bloy, Sheffield Industrial Mission, 1984

13. "Report of the Sub-Committee appointed to confer, in regard to the Thursday Evening Group, on worship and instruction in the Christian Faith." Undated [1953/4]

14. Conference Report, September 1951

15. *Mission Meetings: a sketch of the work of the Sheffield Industrial Mission in the fifties and sixties,* Philip Bloy, Sheffield Industrial Mission, 1984, p.7

16. Interview with Mr S.M. de Bartolome

17. "The Origins, Context and Ideology of Industrial Mission 1875-1975", E.H. Lurkins, unpublished PhD thesis, London School of Economics, 1981, pp.171,172, n23

18. Minutes of a Conference held at Whirlow Grange, 12-13.11.55

19. "Out of Sheffield, A personal account of the work of the Sheffield Industrial Mission by one of its missioners", Margaret Kane, Unpublished typescript, n/d [1966/67], pp.50-51

20. *Church and People in an Industrial Society,* E.R. Wickham, Lutterworth, 1957, p.267

21. "Industrial Mission", L.S. Hunter, unpublished late typescript

22. Report of the Steel Peech and Tozer Industrial Mission Annual General Meeting, 20.5.58

23. The name and the ethos were borrowed from the national Christian Frontier Council, which published a quarterly journal, *Frontier,* and was actively supported by such people as Joe Oldham, Alec Vidler, and Mark Gibbs.

24. *Church and People in an Industrial Society,* E.R. Wickham, Lutterworth, 1957. This was the premiss on which he opened the book: Introduction, p.11

25. Wickham was never an ecumenist. Denominational differences were irrelevant in the works, and also in Wickham's approach. He welcomed any who shared his vision. See "The Origins, Context and Ideology of Industrial Mission 1875-1975", E.H. Lurkins, unpublished PhD thesis, London School of Economics, 1981, p.176, n57

26. See also, E.R. Wickham, "What should be the new look?", in: *The English Church, A New Look,* L.S.Hunter (ed.), Penguin, 1966, pp.144-167

27. *Ministry without Portfolio,* Colin Cuttell, Toc H, 1962, p.77

28. See, *Priests and Workers: An Anglo-French Discussion,* D.L. Edwards (ed.), SCM, 1961

29. In the judgement of Patrick Vaughan one consequence of this dispute was further delay of discussion on a potential non-stipendiary ministry. See, "Historical Background", in, *Non-Stipendiary Ministry in the Church of England,* Mark Hodge, Church Information Office, 1983

30. *The Church and Industry. An interpretation of each to the other. An assessment of the need and the response so far made. Suggestions for advance,* British Council of Churches, January 1958

31. *The Task of the Church in Relation to Industry,* A Report prepared by a Working Party of the Social and Industrial Council, The Church Information Office, 1959, C.A. 1288

32. " 'Workers' Bishop stays in industry", L.S. Hunter, *Sheffield Star,* 13.10.58

33. "Industrial Mission", L.S. Hunter, unpublished late typescript

3

CONSOLIDATION AND DISARRAY, 1960-1968

1960-1963, The calm before the storm

When Wickham left, Michael Jackson stepped into his shoes.

Jackson's interest in industrial mission work had begun ten years earlier while he was at Cambridge University. He had spent the summer of 1949 in France where he was gripped by the example of the French worker-priests. On his return he made contact with Leslie Hunter who came to Cambridge and spoke to a meeting at the University. Jackson attended the first theological students' course in the summer of 1950. He had just graduated and he decided to remain in Sheffield working on the shop floor of stainless steel makers, Firth Vickers.

A year later Jackson went from Sheffield to Wells to train for the priesthood. Towards the end of his training, Wickham contacted him to offer him the chance to become a worker-priest. Hunter had negotiated permission from his fellow bishops for an experimental worker-priest scheme. Because it was an experiment ordination would not take place immediately. As with Wickham in 1944, Jackson's first task was to spend time on the shop floor simply to discover whether the circumstances might arise in which Hunter would feel confident to ordain him deacon, or even priest, while he remained a worker. In 1953 he began work at specialist steel makers, Firth Brown's. After two years some of the workers, on their own account, approached the Bishop to suggest ordination. Hunter concurred and Jackson was ordained deacon. He continued to work on the shop floor for a further 18 months before joining the Mission full time. No-one else joined Jackson in this particular experiment in Sheffield's industry.

A foreman at Firth Brown's recalled Jackson clearly,

"He was a big chap, tended to be on the heavy side, and yet he was young, fit. He was pale faced, and yet you wouldn't call him a weakling. He'd glasses, fairish hair, a little on the curly side.

"He was on the pit side, and the pit side took in various jobs, from sweeping the place up for a start, to preparing moulds, heads, setting pits, to team down, because Firth Brown's was a special steel division and very little top pouring was done, it was

mostly uphill pouring – down a trumpet – so that he was the
general labourer for your first hand pit-man, [one of a number] ...
shovelling muck, because biggest part of a melting job is work in
muck.

"I were quite interested, I couldn't really understand his
position there. Whether to treat him as something with kid gloves,
or whether to do as everyone seemed to do, swear at him ... which
I thought was rather strange in front of a man of God. ... But then
I realised he was just that little cut above the usual. He spoke
different, he seemed to think deeper, and yet he was aloof, ... But
I liked the fellow, he was alright."[1]

When Jackson took over from Wickham change was in the air in industry
and in the nation at large. New working practices were coming in. Managers
were increasingly professional and qualified. There was a steady growth of
intermediate (foreman, supervisor, technician) grades, and a reduction in the
number and proportion of shop-floor workers. Mechanisation was growing
and was combined with changing shift patterns which reduced the slack spells
of work that chaplains had found so useful. Further afield, the early sixties
appeared to belong to youth, to novelty, and to loud, irreverent pop music.
Churches experimented with liturgy; new translations of the Bible appeared;
and the Second Vatican Council revealed that even the most conservative and
hierarchical of denominations was vulnerable to the infectious atmosphere of
liberalisation. For Jackson the fact of change, and the need of the Mission to
respond to it, was an important source of his own concern to look again at the
way the Mission worked.

It is never easy to succeed a charismatic founder and leader of any
organisation and Jackson laboured under the additional handicap that Bishop
Hunter was not entirely happy with the appointment. Hunter appointed three
Senior Friends of the Mission to offer occasional, external oversight of the
development of the Mission. They were the Archdeacon of Sheffield, Robin
Woods, Gerald Hollis, a long standing friend of the Mission, and Frank
Hone, Vicar of Attercliffe. All were members of the Bishop's Advisory
Committee on Industrial Mission, though Hone had only joined it earlier in
1959. Some of the chaplains saw their intervention as distracting from the
work of mission; they certainly detracted from Jackson's authority as the new
leader.

There was an almost complete turnover in the staff of the Mission.
Margaret Kane joined in April 1959 and Brian Cordingly began full time in
October 1959. Michael Atkinson, and Ian MacKay arrived in 1960; and John

Rhodes in 1961. The first Free Church chaplain, Congregationalist Barry Parker, was appointed in 1962. Most of Wickham's staff left: Philip Bloy went to West Africa, Bill Matthews moved to a parish in Leicester, and John Rogan to staff the Industry Committee of the Board for Social Responsibility, the muted legacy of Wickham's campaign for a national Industrial Mission Secretariat. Secondments swelled the team. Frank Scuffham spent two years in Sheffield and returned to Peterborough in September 1962. David Lee came from South Wales for six months in 1960, and from October 1962 Graham Bride came for a year from Melbourne, Australia.

In Sheffield the new team worked well together. They shared a loose collegiality based on close team work, on joint visiting in the same works, and on a strong social life together. Once a month team meetings included "Reith Lectures": theological or sociological papers given by each member of staff for debate amongst themselves. Chaplains knew that they were at the leading edge of mission and of the accompanying theological exploration and they relished the task.

At least as important as internal staff changes was the retirement of Bishop Hunter in March 1962. SIM had been heavily reliant on his experience and his patronage. But in the final three years of his episcopacy Hunter began to demand of Jackson things he had not demanded of Wickham. When, he wanted to know, was the bridge into industry to see people travelling across it into the Churches? Hunter had always accepted the argument that it would be a long time before the Mission brought forth visible results, and he had protected the Mission from its early critics on these grounds. Yet after more than 15 years the harvest seemed disappointingly meagre.

Between 1959 and 1962 the originator, builder, and most experienced members of staff all departed the area. Only Michael Jackson remained of the team Wickham had built. Nevertheless all the new staff were committed to continue the work of the previous 15 years. Margaret Kane had been closely associated with the Mission for seven years during her parochial ministry at Maltby, outside Rotherham. Brian Cordingly, and Michael Atkinson had come to Sheffield in order to work with Wickham, and had worked part time with SIM whilst serving as curates in nearby parishes.

Hunter's successor was John Taylor, an evangelical academic, with a background in theological education and lacking experience of ministry in industrial areas. Taylor was viewed with anxiety by the staff. There was resentment when Jackson alone was invited to his enthronement. Taylor's understanding of the Church was a conceptual world away from that of the chaplains. He saw the Church as an elect community, sent through no virtue of its own for the benefit of the world. His approach was couched in terms of authority and discipline and the Lordship of Christ.[2] This was perhaps reflected in his relationship with the chaplains. Where Hunter had known them individually, and exercised episcopal control directly, Taylor dealt with the Mission through Jackson. He saw Jackson as a vicar, and the chaplains as his curates. Some were convinced that the new Bishop had arrived with the intention of undoing SIM, and other initiatives of his predecessor, but this was nervous speculation. Though it was too big and too well known to have been a matter of indifference, there is no evidence that the Mission was of major concern to Taylor until circumstances forced the Mission on him.[3] But the atmosphere in the Diocese had changed dramatically, and Taylor did not offer the Mission the support and backing necessary for it to thrive.

Ted Wickham, now in Manchester, had not given up his campaign for a national co-ordinated industrial mission structure. In 1961 he joined the Industry Committee of the Board for Social Responsibility as its Deputy Chairman, and he continued to try to push the Church of England towards his vision of an Industrial Mission Secretariat, though perhaps without great expectations of success.

The remaining official structure open to him was the Church and Industry Sub-committee of the Social Responsibility Department of the British Council of Churches. This group included Wickham and Jackson, Tom Chapman and Richard O'Brien representing the Church of England, the Baptist C.H. Cleal, Bill Gowland for the Methodists, and representatives of the Church of Scotland, the Presbyterian Church and the Congregationalists. Together they constituted the initiators and leaders of industrial mission in each of the major denominations of the BCC. The intention was that they would together plan and guide the ecumenical development of industrial mission. However their powers were limited to the ability to recommend good practice to denominational authorities locally and nationally, and as this collection of strong willed men held profoundly divergent views agreement was not easy to achieve.

Wickham's main instrument for guiding industrial mission was a group of chaplains gathered together in what became known as the "Axis" meetings. The name stemmed from his letter of invitation which suggested that meeting would lead to the "strengthening of a common theological axis between us". The first meeting, in February 1960, comprised 11 present or past members of SIM, and five others, including Simon Phipps from Coventry, Ralph Stevens from Birmingham, and a visitor from Japan. At its first meeting Wickham analysed the weakness of industrial mission nationally, and thus the nature of the challenge the group faced. It was materially fragile, and too often dependent on the goodwill of an individual bishop. There were too few chaplains, and ecclesiastical tokenism was reflected in isolated appointments. Work was often qualitatively weak and "messy". More serious still was the confusion of purpose which stemmed from the influx of chaplains of varied theological perspectives. Whether they were conventionally churchy, conservatively evangelical, Methodist minded industrial evangelists, or simply inadequate Anglicans, all detracted from the ultimate tasks of industrial mission.[4] Wickham intended the group to become the theological driving force of industrial mission nationally, but as a voluntary association it lacked sufficient strength. The group met twice a year, its membership grew steadily, and it drifted into a congenial discussion group.

When Jackson took over as Senior Chaplain the Mission was stronger than ever. But its strength was Wickham's legacy, not Jackson's creation. An inevitable time-lag meant that the Mission was living off the reputation it had built up in the 1950s. New staff, secondees, and the Mission's international standing all reflected work that was past. There were those opposed to Sheffield and all it stood for, but they were few and disparate voices against the strong, articulate and dynamic new team of chaplains. Yet Jackson could not afford to rest on Wickham's laurels. To sustain the work in Sheffield, and to keep SIM's external profile high, demanded that he build on the organisation he had inherited, and that he impress his own mark upon it.

Continuity was the watchword on Wickham's departure. A staff review in 1960, with Bishop Hunter present, charted the development of work to that point. Apart from a concern that the Mission had never effectively addressed the "roughest" of shop floor workers, it reaffirmed the basic lines of approach. Works visiting and discussion meetings still dominated the chaplains' working day. Eight chaplains covered 18 steel and engineering companies in Sheffield and Rotherham, and some departments of British Rail. An estimated 250 lay groups were meeting, of which 20 were considered full "lay projects". A number of companies sustained strong networks of meetings. In several firms chaplains were involved in training apprentices, in company induction courses, and in management and foreman training. Five or six conferences were held each year attended by around 150 people. The annual theological students' course continued, although in 1960 Ridley Hall decided to send students to a rival scheme set up for its students by Michael Brooke in Manchester. The stream of visitors from all over the world was unabated.

Local progress often had national connections. Work in British Rail, for example, which had begun in Sheffield in 1958, grew steadily through the 1960s. In 1962 there were 13 monthly groups running. Maximum attendance at most of them was between 10 and 20, though the Mission seemed particularly attractive with the wages staff: they had one group with up to 36 people attending, and another with up to 80. In 1962 the observation was made that

> "It is also rather difficult to assess what types of individual really attend the meetings because they feel they really benefit. Some unquestionably come out of curiosity and one or two to see what capital they can make out of it from the Management v. Trade Union point of view . . . It is considered, generally, that the movement does a great deal of good in spite of the suspicion with which some regard it. There is a tendency at meetings to discuss anything but religion. Perhaps this is a good thing and indirectly serves our purpose."[5]

The railway industry was in a difficult period of contraction. In the Sheffield Division alone employment in British Rail fell from around 12,000 in 1958 to 7,000 in 1968. Regular, twice-yearly, national meetings of rail chaplains were convened. They were addressed by senior members of the national management and unions. Speakers included Sir Brian (later Lord) Robertson, Chairman of the British Transport Commission, and Sidney Green, General Secretary of the National Union of Railwaymen. Both men were also members of the Church of England's Industry Committee. The chaplains' role in these circumstances was ambivalent. A minority wanted to raise questions of justice and good management. In practice these potentially critical voices were few and chaplains used their wider knowledge to help ease the processes of change, either through the pastoral care of workers, or by encouraging them to take a broader, more managerial view, and therefore to accept inevitable change more readily.

There were significant developments in the lay leadership of the Mission. In 1959 the Sunday Lay Leaders' meeting set up a small sub-committee to run its work, and also, after considerable debate, elected a lay chairman to replace the previous clerical leadership. They stressed that this was not a response to the change in staff, but a development that had been planned for some time. However, Wickham's departure and the relatively inexperienced new staff put even more onus on this development to succeed. It was a tangible step forward in the laicisation of the Mission, and some of the leaders began to talk about a time when they would work chaplains out of a job.

At the same time there was a pressure to codify the thinking of the Mission in relation to the laity. In 1960 a group began work on "A Lay-man's manual, The Training of Laymen, and Lay-work Propaganda".[6] Various drafts of papers on these themes were discussed amongst the lay leaders and the chaplains over the following couple of years. Considerable stress was placed on the personal qualities of a lay leader. They should be familiar with changing industry, and be a source of confidence, imagination, and vision. They were to "out-think" their social group, while remaining part of it. There was an acceptance that lay leaders played different roles as a consequence of their position in industry: the opportunities and the restrictions were different for the shop-floor worker, office staff, or the company director. A modification of the meaning of the term "lay leader" was observed. It had applied to those who led industrial mission groups. It came to be applied also to those who, from an industrial mission perspective, took a leading role in industry, politics, or social life, even where they led no group.

Lay groups were codified according to the degree of involvement of the lay leader. Groups were:

(a) those which the chaplain convened and ran;
(b) those which remained the responsibility of the chaplain, but where one person accepted responsibility for convening the meeting (these lay leaders were known to the chaplains as "sheepdogs");
(c) a meeting drawn from a particular social or industrial grouping which met regularly, outside working hours, still with a chaplain;
(d) a similar meeting, but wholly led by one of the lay people in the group. The chaplain's only role was as occasional visiting speaker.[7]

Most emphasis was placed on the second and third groups. The first implied no lay leadership, and the fourth was rare. The fourth stage was still not the final objective of the Mission, but only the beginning of a Christian group. Once formed it still had to grow secure and solid, while at the same time being open to change, and even to splitting into more groups. This was not an easy process, but it was exciting.

But by the time agreement was emerging on these ideas, they were almost anachronistic. By 1961 Jackson had decided on a new direction for the Mission, though he did not announce it in so many words. In a handwritten note to himself Jackson jotted down,

"1. Theological and policy shift

"from indigenous industrial Church to Kingdom of God – policy of industrial penetration, dialogue and research"[8]

Industrial penetration had been achieved – though a great deal more was still possible. *Dialogue and research* became the key concepts of the new approach. These were the means by which Christian insights and principles could be brought to bear on the rapidly changing industrial world. This policy shift did not amount to a violent switch of direction, but by emphasising certain aspects of the Mission's activity, and downgrading others, notably the para-church, it did constitute a significant change in the character of the Mission.

There were a number of immediate implications of this policy shift. Not least was Jackson's desire to reduce the tendency towards a centralised hierarchical structure for SIM, and to replace it by a more dispersed pattern of activity. This would curtail the growing power of the lay leaders in the Mission, and strengthen Jackson's own position.

Jackson set out his proposals on the direction that SIM should take at the 1963 Lay Leaders' Conference. He asked how the Mission could reach those who knew nothing about it, even in companies where there was a chaplain? And he contrasted the central organisation of lay leaders in Sheffield with a more dispersed company-based organisation, such as in Steel Peech and Tozer. The conference was ambivalent on the first question, observing that it was sometimes difficult to distinguish industrial mission groups from others. It did, however, broadly endorse Jackson's preference for company-based lay organisations over the central meetings, though the issue was referred back to the lay leaders for further discussion. Jackson's closing summary charted the way forward:

> "the Christian mission could be said to involve the development of
> a proper knowledge of the world and of industrial society and how
> it operated. To express concern for it, to develop expressions of
> love in it, and to try to see what men could and should be."[9]

Jackson elaborated these views in a later article in the *International Review of Missions*:

> "What is our present situation? On the industrial side one of
> continuing technological *change*, bringing re-organisation to com-
> panies, new patterns of labour force, new types of industrial work
> within it. Some of these factors are general to all companies,
> others are particular in individual companies. The other factor in
> our situation is an open *debate* about how we should express our
> response, and how we should understand the basic Christian ideas.

The frontier between technological change and theological debate is, therefore, a difficult one for laymen and chaplains, which means that much of our work is in the nature of *research* rather than working from clearly agreed principles, and that our thinking and our organisation need to be flexible."[10]

Yet despite this conference, and other occasions on which Jackson set out his ideas, it is not clear that this shift and the extent of its implications were evident to the other chaplains nor to the lay people involved. They were aware of a change in tenor, perhaps a greater emphasis on the intellect, but these were simply ascribed to a change in personality. It still seemed to most people in the Mission that SIM continued to build faithfully on the foundations Wickham had laid down. In 1964, for example, Michael Atkinson wrote,

"we find ourselves, after twenty years of history, still comparatively close to the pattern projected by Bishop Hunter in the early days of his episcopate."[11]

Indeed, most work continued as it always had. Wickham had always talked about secular issues in secular terms, and had encouraged both lay people and chaplains to take an ever deeper interest in public affairs, and to be able to offer well grounded critiques of industrial and social issues. Regular works visiting continued, although changing work patterns had reduced the number of opportunities for shop-floor meetings. Atkinson estimated that SIM was in touch with 43,000 out of 70,000 workers in the works they visited.[12] Chaplains met and talked with people at all levels in industry from director to cleaner. Pastoral work remained important. Meetings outside work continued, as did the Thursday Evening Group and the lay leaders' organisations.

Yet, despite all that was the same, Jackson's subtle shift in perspective was basic. For Wickham industry had been the subject, and Christianity the object of mission. Under Jackson the relationship was reversed. Christianity became the subject and industry the object of mission. Despite all the years he had spent working in and ministering to industry Jackson stood theologically, as it were, outside looking in.

The change of direction was strongest in the change of ethos of the "lay project". "Lay projects" had been a synonym for the groups which would comprise the para-church. Now the term became interchangeable with "study group". The use of the same phrase further disguised the shift in the destination of the Mission. Instead of the para-church the destination of Sheffield Industrial Mission became, in Jackson's eyes at least, the furthering of the Kingdom of God primarily through the application of Christianity to industry and its problems. The nature of the Kingdom of God was expressed by Paul Tillich's idea of the "theonomy" in which the relationship between God and society is such that society has its own autonomous existence, and the holy, the spiritual, is directly visible in that autonomy. Theonomy affirms the autonomous creative processes of society, and is in permanent struggle against the tendency of the Church, and others, to define and control what is holy.[13]

Dialogue and research were routes towards the Kingdom of God, and the primary tool open to the Mission was the development of lay projects or study groups. Again, study groups were not new in themselves. The Management Group, for example, had long worked in this way. Between 1957 and 1960 it had addressed: payment; working hours and shift work; participation in industry; the social aims of industry; and both the recession (in 1958) and the affluent society (in 1960). In 1961 Jackson suggested to them that these internal studies could be built on through written reports, discussion with other groups, short conferences on a topic, or large meetings with speakers of national reputation. What was new was the emphasis placed upon study as the primary means by which industrial mission was to be pursued.

The energies of SIM, and in particular of its most committed members, were increasingly focused on studies of pressing social and industrial issues. In 1963 the Mission joined a joint consultation on "The Industrial Situation in the North of England" with prepared papers from industrialists, trades unionists, and industrial chaplains. In 1964 groups produced reports on city planning; work and leisure; and control in industry. The Rotherham Lay Leaders Study Group, drawn from Steel Peech and Tozer studied "Some Patterns of Employment in Advanced Industrial Society". In September 1964 a conference was held on "The Clerical Worker Today" which brought together white collar workers from local firms and parishes.

Study groups worked in wholly secular terms. Some then added an explicitly Christian commentary or reflection. For most, however, the contribution of Christianity lay implicit in the ability to approach a topic at a deeper or more critical level than was conventionally possible, or in the openness with which groups approached their topics, or in the general optimism of their conclusions. One consequence was that it became hard to distinguish Industrial Mission groups from similar groups in industry or academia, or to distinguish Christian from secular thought.

Jackson's policy shift was also reflected in a growing emphasis placed on the "frontier" as the location of industrial mission, and on the "ministry to the structures". Chaplains began to put more time into meetings with those involved in local politics, trades unions, employers' associations and other agencies whose decisions influenced the nature of local society. The Frontier Groups were perhaps the most formal expression of this interest. The Sheffield Frontier Group met between 1959 and 1964. Its programme of speakers addressed many aspects of public life: the welfare state; education; democracy; scientific developments; town planning. There were also talks on Christian principles and beliefs in public life. Invitations to these meetings were carefully controlled and attendance varied between eight and 20. In them the Mission sought to provide a neutral meeting place in which chaplains could raise some of the deeper questions exposed by these discussions. A careful distinction was maintained between chaplains' personal political commitment and the need for the Church to retain its political independence and objectivity, though this was a distinction which could be hard to sustain in a public setting.

The idea of the frontier was the inverse of that of the gulf. Instead of focusing on the divide between the Church and the world which had to be bridged, the frontier stressed the mutual border, the common ground where the world and the Church met. The frontier was therefore where the laity lived out their Christianity.

Both gulf and frontier were important notions. The gulf between the institutional Church and the institutions of secular life was patently visible in the marginalisation of the Churches. Lay discipleship in the world was perfunctory or, more often, absent. The explanation of this state of affairs, and thus also the key to amending it, was philosophical: the conceptual world of Christianity, its theology, had become incomprehensible to secular systems of thought. Therefore the chaplains' frontier task was to rebuild the connection between Christian and secular understandings. Accepting secular systems of thought as given, they sought to re-evaluate Christian theology, and they worked together on a secular theology that would be adequate to the needs of frontier mission.

In 1963 Michael Jackson, Margaret Kane, Ian Mackay and Michael Atkinson collaborated on a book entitled *Christian Mission in Industry*.[14] It addressed this frontier and distilled much of SIM's experience and reflections. It never saw the light of day. Jackson had last minute doubts about its suitability for publication and consulted, amongst others, Ted Wickham and Bishop Hunter. On their advice he stopped the project though it was already at the stage of page proofs and due for publication by Lutterworth in 1964.

In the book Jackson presented Industrial Mission as an agency of the Church which addressed the dominant, normative structures of society. These were industry, and linked bodies like trades unions, research associations, government departments, and educational establishments. He set out three aims for the mission. The first was the good society: open (as delineated by Karl Popper), secular, pluralist, tolerant, and theonomous (as elaborated by Paul Tillich), where ultimate meaning is visible through everyday thought and action. The second aim was a good industrial order in which the good society is present, and in which industry serves society. The third aim was to build up a body of men to take this vision forward. No longer was SIM focused on bridging any gulf. This was the statement of an organisation sure of its lodgement in industry and in public affairs, and which was setting out to make a difference to the world.

The task of the laity was to work prophetically at the frontier of Christian belief and industrial or political action. Lay projects offered the means to study common problems in the light of Christian beliefs. The ultimate aim of these projects was not knowledge, but the application of the groups' findings. In this way industry would be permeated, stained, with Christian principles. Jackson estimated that there were then some 500 lay people actively associated with the mission, though few attended Churches.[15] The chaplains' role was to encourage the development of such lay leadership. Although the Church as an institution had been defeated by secularism, industrial mission held out the possibility of re-establishing an old relationship between Church and society in a new way. Hooker's conception of the unity of Church and State could be replaced by the perception that the Christian faith was coterminous with human activity. The Anglican nature of this vision is left implicit.

Kane addressed some of the industrial issues of the early 1960s. Her approach was factual and sociological, and she was able to draw on the explorations and findings of many of the Mission's study groups. She drew particular attention to questions of automation and to redundancies in industries which had traditionally been big employers. There is a Christian background to her discussion of industrial issues, which is referred to, but which for most of the discussion is left implicit and highly generalised.

It fell to Mackay and Atkinson to address the core philosophical issue of how Christian faith could make sense in a secular context. Their starting assumption was the inadequacy of traditional Christian language. Christian words did not make sense, and Christian ideas had lost their power and substance for those who lived and worked in a wholly secular world. Thereafter they parted company. Mackay held a more existentialist position in which theology was a discourse which drew its potency from the individual Christian whose life and involvement in society gave substance to the concepts of freedom and reason. A Christian social ethic adequate to a secular society could not be based on a metaphysical appeal; it had to be grounded on the engagement of Christians with society. This echoed the emphasis the Mission laid on the personal qualities of its lay leaders.

Atkinson asserted that traditional theological language did have a role in safeguarding Christian orthodoxy, though it had no place in mission or apologetics. But for him it was not Christian terminology, but Christian commitment that was too narrow. Through its history the Church had, he asserted, sought to dominate society or had retreated into individualist piety. Yet SIM had a theological understanding and method which avoided this false dichotomy and which brought the secular and the Christian back together. The doctrine of creation asserted that the whole world belonged to God, not just the community of Christians. Though people have rebelled, God will ultimately prevail. Through the incarnation, and Jesus' life and work, God's Kingdom has broken into human life. Christian discipleship lay in the service of both God and humanity. Industrial mission worked to encourage such discipleship amongst those who called themselves Christian and those who did not. Religious ideas could not simply be presented to people raw and untranslated. "Middle axioms", however, offered a method by which Christian concepts could be translated, however inadequately, into terms that secularised people understood: for example, love, mercy, truth, compassion, and justice. Once people understood that Christianity was concerned with these issues, they would begin to explore their religious depths. Similarly, if the Church understood itself in appropriate terms – as both an historically conditioned body of believers, and also as continuously led by the Spirit into new forms – then as an institution it too could once again engage with the secular world.

The chaplains were not pursuing these themes in a vacuum. In the late 1950s and 1960s many theologians, Wickham amongst them, explored the issues of secular theology. At first they sought for ways by which the immutable Truth of the Christian Gospel could be heard by modern, secular people. They recast the Christian message in new words, and they cut out what they saw as ecclesiastical or primitive ways of thinking. But excising mythological or supernatural ideas from theology also seemed to strip Christianity of its essential metaphysical core. God, it seemed, was outmoded. It also implied that external, secular change affected the content and process of theology. If this was so then Christianity was culturally relative and any claim to God's Truth which stood outside time and space was invalid.

The absolutism of theology, including the absolutism of the first phase of secular theologians, was therefore no longer tenable. For some this was exhilarating. For others the same logic revealed only the destructive nature of secular theology. Because, they asserted, the Truth of the Gospel is timeless, those who sought to undermine it from within were apostate.

The book was not published and it is impossible to judge how it would have been received. However, in March 1963 the Bishop of Woolwich, John Robinson, had published *Honest to God*[16] and publicised it with an article in *The Observer*. The book was short, readable, and powerful. Its content was not novel. Its impact lay in the fact that a bishop was popularising a theological debate in a way which touched a popular nerve, and theological debate was suddenly public property. The term "secular theology" entered common parlance. Some detractors asserted that while such discussions were tolerable in theological cloisters, in public they were a scandal to the faith. Journalists, clergy, and theologians commented at length whether or not they had understood the Bishop.

The underlying battle was between traditional faith and radical and dangerous innovation. Wickham and SIM were explicitly aligned with Robinson and the secular theologians. Wickham was acknowledged by name in *Honest to God*, and also in Paul van Buren's *The Secular Meaning of the Gospel*.[17] Traditionalists charged John Robinson with heresy, atheism, undermining the faith and the Church, and with encouraging immorality amongst the young. Robinson's public defence of *Lady Chatterley's Lover* in the book's highly publicised obscenity trial only served to prove the latter point.[18] Those who stood by traditional values, the unchanging verities of the faith and the timeless authority of the Church, felt betrayed and beleaguered. They fought back.

In the works chaplains took the explosion of media interest in theology as a heaven-sent opportunity for debate and discussion. Jackson, however, grew less and less happy with events. Wickham's shoes, which had begun to pinch very early, now no longer fitted him at all.

1964-1966, Troubles

From the autumn of 1963 friction began to surface in SIM.[19]

Small incidents, fraught meetings, and disparaging statements started to roll around the team like grit in the bearings. Jackson doubted the quality of chaplains' work; staff questioned his autocratic manner. One episode revealed the deterioration of relationships. In the spring of 1965 Jackson suggested an the inclusion of lay leaders in the chaplains' meetings. This was opposed by the staff. Nevertheless Jackson asked a group of lay people, led by Ron Stevens, to review SIM and to offer advice on its policies. It was to report directly to him, and its terms of reference included issues of recruitment and deployment of staff. The staff discovered the review group through a chance remark while Jackson was on holiday in India. In his absence resentment was vocalised. Margaret Kane was delegated to demand more open debate from the Senior Chaplain. The review duly proposed an extended staff meeting, in which lay people and chaplains would together establish the Mission's policy. Chaplains resented this incursion into what they regarded as their domain: the lay nature of the Mission, they argued, was Christian ministry in the works, not the administration of SIM. Chaplains accused Jackson of using the group to extend his own authority. He retorted by accusing them of mediocrity and clericalism. They continued their opposition.

In late spring or early summer 1965 Jackson had a fundamental change of heart. His dissatisfaction with secular theology was converted, apparently suddenly, to a thorough-going traditionalist orthodoxy and ecclesiastical authoritarianism. He had changed sides. His conversion could only sow confusion in the Mission.

The crisis was precipitated at the annual two-day staff conference at the end of August 1965. Contrary to previous practice Jackson dominated the meeting, giving all but one of the papers, and setting out in explicit terms both his new theological position and his authority as Senior Chaplain. The staff felt bewildered and betrayed. Jackson was committing them to a traditional theological stance utterly at variance with what Wickham had taught and the position they had held since joining the Mission. Furthermore he was tying this new theological position to loyalty to himself. Staff were given no space to debate either the theology or the process of change. They were in effect faced with an ultimatum: support Jackson and traditional theology, or leave the Mission.

Ian Mackay protested in writing to Jackson. In mid-September 1965 Jackson gave Mackay twelve months' notice, and Parker three months, which he later extended to a year. Both protested that their dismissals were abrupt, arbitrary, lacking any proper consultation process, and that they were given no adequate reason. The Congregational Union was informed of Parker's dismissal. It had not been consulted. Both men exercised their right to see Bishop Taylor to ask for reinstatement, but the Bishop backed his Senior Chaplain. Jackson himself, seeing that a storm was brewing, asked Taylor whether he should withdraw the notices of dismissal, but the Bishop endorsed his action and was ready for any protest.

Relations in the team had clearly broken down past the point of reparability. SIM was split in two. Differences of theological opinion or views on the development of the Mission within the team became irrelevant. Staff and laity were forced to take sides. Jackson was supported by Bishop Taylor and other senior members of the Church, along with some lay people. Parker and Mackay were supported by most of their colleagues, most of the lay leadership of the Mission, and the more radical wing of the Church. Jackson stood on his authority as Senior Chaplain, and the need to improve the quality of the work. Parker and Mackay believed that they were victimised for their theological beliefs. Each side raised questions central to the nature and theology of mission, but conflict drowned out rational debate.

Jackson's basic charge against both Parker and Mackay was that they had lost their way. They were well integrated in the works, but they had forgotten that the point of being there was to convey the Christian Gospel to their listeners. They had crossed the gulf so far that they had, as it were, "gone native"; identification with the industry had been bought at the price of losing Christian distinctiveness. Access to the works, discussion groups and conferences had ceased to be methods of mission and had become ends in themselves. Yet Jackson did not articulate this accusation clearly at the time; it was confused in a welter of criticism of the chaplains' poor grasp of doctrine, of mediocre theology, and absent spirituality. He accused staff of being vulnerable to industrial pressure groups, in particular to the trades unions. He asserted that they had departed from the true catholic faith to establish an industrial mission sect. Other chaplains in the team protested that the evidence against Parker and Mackay could equally well be laid against any of them, and therefore it was unfair to pick on these two.

The following month, October 1965, Jackson was due to begin 12 months' study leave, though he intended to remain in Sheffield. SIM was given into the joint charge of Magaret Kane and Michael Atkinson. These two, in addition to a sympathy for their sacked colleagues, faced the problem of responding to rumours of dismissals and conflict which were already whipping around the works. Kane and Atkinson therefore offered to reinstate the two sacked chaplains. Bishop Taylor abruptly informed them that they did not have this power. They resigned as leaders. Jackson was recalled to post. It was clear to Parker and Mackay that appeals through official channels would be ineffective. Therefore they faced a choice between acquiescence and departure, or resistance and a fight. They consulted a number of people, including Ted Wickham in Manchester, and decided to stay. They used the only weapon to hand, an "appeal to Sheffield", rallying supporters in Sheffield's industry and trades unions to apply such pressure on the Bishop that they would be reinstated and Jackson be dismissed in their stead.

In November 1965 an article in the *New Christian* magazine about the chaplains' dismissals was reprinted the following day in the local evening paper, *The Sheffield Star*. From then on the mission's troubles were public property.[20] The row was the subject of increasing media interest, including editorials in *The Times* and *The Guardian*.[21]

News of the dismissals provoked an immediate response from lay members of SIM. Managers, trades unionists, and shop-floor workers were swift to point to hypocrisy. For years the Mission had taught that workers should be treated with respect on both an organisational and a personal level. Yet Jackson had exercised his power like an old-time owner-manager, with no consideration of good employment practice. Jackson further compounded the problem by refusing to discuss the matter in public, being very reluctant to talk about it in private, and not countenancing mediation. As far as he was concerned both what he had done and the way he had done it were entirely proper. The recruitment, deployment, and dismissal of staff were matters for him and the Bishop alone as the sole ecclesiastical authorities in the matter.

If Jackson dug himself into a hole, Bishop Taylor handed him fresh shovels. Some of Sheffield's most powerful industrialists tried to defuse the crisis through prompt intervention. The Bishop told them that the decisions had been taken in the best interests of SIM, and there were no grounds for consultation. A further approach was made to him by a delegation of shop stewards and senior managers. Their visit was resented and the delegation haughtily dismissed.

The body which might have been expected to take the lead in resolving the issues, the Bishop's Advisory Committee on Industrial Mission, was as much in the dark as anyone else. In October 1965 its secretary, a trades union representative, asked the Bishop to call an emergency meeting. His request was refused. The Committee met only twice during the dispute and became another battleground, not least because some staff members were also members of the Committee. It took considerable pressure before Jackson was prepared to discuss the dismissal of two of his staff with the Committee. When he did so he spread out his charges against the two men. He also, for the first time, set out a comprehensive critique of Wickham's approach to mission, characterising it as sectarian and clerical. Bishop Taylor, chairing the meeting, would accept no criticism of the Senior Chaplain and the meeting broke up in disarray. At the subsequent meeting Gerald Hollis successfully moved a vote of no confidence in the Bishop.

Taylor was an episcopal absolutist. He stressed the Lordship of Christ, and the consequent invulnerability of Christ's servants to external criticism. The task of the chaplain, he asserted, was that of any minister. It was to be a "man of God", witnessing in his own person to the Lordship of Christ over all of life, including industry. Therefore the Church, and the Church alone, must exercise authority about where and how its ministers serve, entirely independent of outside pressures.[22]

But the pressures were also internal. The vicissitudes of the Mission were grist to the mill of the already unhappy internal diocesan politics. Rotherham Deanery Chapter voted to support the sacked men, and the Archdeacon of Doncaster actively took up their cause. Informal contacts spread news of the dispute widely and efficiently, if not always accurately. This was a battle between radicals and traditionalists and people entirely separate from the disputants took sides on the issues.

Informal and formal approaches reached the Archbishops. In November 1965 a group of managers from four companies wrote to the Archbishops of York and Canterbury. The following April a delegation travelled to York to see Donald Coggan, to request an enquiry into events in the Mission, and to ask him to call on Bishop Wickham to retrieve the situation before it was too late. Wickham made clear his opposition to the direction Jackson was taking. He thought that Jackson should go, and declared that he could restore the Mission and confidence in it in short order. An enquiry was instituted, but neither Coggan nor Taylor would tolerate Wickham's involvement.

In fact two official enquiries were established. In March 1966 a working party was set up under the leadership of Mr H.P. (Tim) Forder. Its terms of reference were

> "to inquire into the future of the Sheffield Industrial Mission, to examine its aims, its theological basis, its relation to industry and the Church and any matters of organisation."[23]

It was to enquire into the mistakes of Mission's past, but it was not to address the present troubles. It reported in May 1967 and largely set the tone for the reconstruction of the Mission (see below, pp.68–9).

Those supporting Parker and Mackay did not see the Forder working party as independent, impartial, or adequate. It was set up by the Bishop of Sheffield and included Michael Jackson and a majority known to support him and his more conservative theology, though they had appointed a token critic. The delegation to the Archbishop of York requested an enquiry which was visibly independent. Coggan appointed Edwin Barker (Secretary of the Church Assembly's Board for Social Responsibility) as its chairman. With him were Tom Chapman (the BSR's Industry Committee Liaison Officer for Industry and the Trades Unions) and Stanley Linsley (Archdeacon of

Cleveland and previously General Director of the Industrial Christian Fellowship). All three stood outside the dispute, but they could also be expected to sympathise with a more traditional approach to theological and ecclesiastical matters.

The Barker enquiry was asked to examine the sacking of Parker and Mackay, to assess SIM's problems, and to identify what help might be necessary. They interviewed 54 people and received considerable documentary evidence. They rejected the idea that the dismissal of Barry Parker and Ian Mackay could have been sudden or unexpected, and concluded that that the Church's authority had been properly and justly exercised. They concurred with Jackson's grounds for his actions and regarded all criticism of the way in which the chaplains had been dismissed as baseless. They held the two men and their advisors, in particular Ted Wickham, fully responsible for the difficulties which had beset the Mission.

The enquiry identified the issues at the heart of what they called "the war in the staff":

> "The assumption is that the Church has lost contact with men in industry. It is necessary to re-establish links with them and Missioners have gone into industry to do this. They are on a razor-edge. They can become identified with the men they meet by becoming like them without influencing them. They can become additional welfare officers, or exercise a personal and pastoral ministry amongst them without any particular reference to industry except as a meeting place. They can be tempted to interfere in the day-to-day running of industry and its related institutions. These are some of the dangers. In addition their work can become "over-against" the Church, developing a distinct orthodoxy leading to sectarianism."[24]

That the chaplains had in fact succumbed to these dangers is left implicit.

The report as a whole was never made public. On the weekend that a brief summary was published Peter Dodd, whom the report criticised, and a Methodist, David Wright, who had not been criticised, were asked to leave. No lessons appear to have been learned from the previous experiences. The Methodists, who had planned to withdraw Wright, were not consulted in advance. Dr Leslie Davison, then General Secretary of the Methodist Home Missions Department, issued an unprecedented press statement[25] declaring that they had no choice but to accept Wright's dismissal, though they could see no reason for it. Richard Baggott, a Methodist who worked one day a week with the Mission, resigned. The Congregational spokesman on Industrial Affairs, Norman Charlton, announced that they had withdrawn all support from the Sheffield Industrial Mission. There had been no consultation on Parker's dismissal, and in fact they had been approached three months earlier to see if a salary rise was in order.[26] Ecumenical relations were damaged for a decade.

The enquiry left a great many questions unanswered. Theological differences between Wickham and Jackson were, they said, an important discussion but one which should have been kept quite separate from employment issues. They made no judgement of Jackson's leadership of the Mission which had brought it to this parlous state, nor of the implicit loss of control by the Church authorities over its agency. They did not consider whether the Mission had a responsibility to model in its own behaviour the standards of employment practice which it had preached to industry. Consultation, a matter they took very seriously, was, they felt, perhaps appropriate for industry, but not for the Church.

The conclusions of the Barker enquiry were definitive. The Mission was an agency of the Church, and the Church hereby reasserted its control. Jackson was exonerated. Bishop Taylor took the decision that sufficient harm had already been done and no further good would come out of publication. It was his decision to make a summary available but otherwise to bury the report.

There was one other, confidential, review of SIM and its potential, which ran alongside the two official enquiries. Jackson invited a friend, John Nurser, Dean of Trinity Hall, Cambridge, and previously curate at Tankersley, Rotherham, to study SIM's relationship with higher education bodies, and to evaluate the possibility of an Industrial Mission Research Institute.

The key assumption of Nurser's report was that religion in the 1960s had lost most of its overtones of class, and consequently there was no longer any need for a special agency to bridge the gap with the industrial working class. Parish clergy might take responsibility for visiting small works and collieries, and thus redress areas that SIM had previously neglected: pastoral care, prayer, and the Bible. Industrial chaplains would retain responsibility for the larger works. Some, however, might adopt a more specialised role, working closely with those in power, especially at times of industrial conflict. They would need to establish trust through a sympathetic manner, intellectual ability, and wide reading. A small Research Institute, of perhaps two full-time staff, might achieve this aim. It would train parish clergy involved in industrial visiting and other industrial chaplains, systematically building up a body of knowledge in the specialised sphere of contemporary mission. SIM might begin by using its existing links with higher education. John Easton was already being supervised at Leeds University in a course of reading before joining SIM as a chaplain.

These proposals were close to Jackson's heart, but they went nowhere.

1967-1968, The aftermath

The shock waves of the dispute spread far beyond Sheffield. A high proportion of chaplains across the country knew the Sheffield team personally. Many had been attracted into industrial mission through Wickham's example, and had first tasted the work in its student courses or longer training. Confidence and clarity of purpose were badly bruised. The division infected the networks by which chaplains kept in touch with one another. Wickham gave up his long campaign to steer the course of industrial mission nationally, and the "Axis" meetings came to an end.

There were positive consequences. Industrial chaplains from Sheffield were dispersed to industrial mission posts elsewhere and several took a leading role in national and international industrial mission affairs. John Rhodes moved to Humberside, Michael Atkinson to Northampton, Peter Dodd to Newcastle, Margaret Kane to Hong Kong. Walter Wilson left to be curate at Attercliffe. Sheffield's troubles also encouraged the formation of the Industrial Mission Association after some two years of discussion. This was a voluntary association of chaplains which became the largest network and policy forum for industrial mission nationally. In at least one team, Teeside, horror at the ecumenical insensitivity of events in Sheffield led to a formal agreement between the denominations concerned on the terms of employment of their chaplains, designed to prevent the possibility of arbitrary dismissals.

Internationally, many of those concerned with urban and industrial mission, saw events as revenge of the Church hierarchy on a project which had challenged them. The parallel with the suppression of the French worker-priest movement was strong. The outcome was a victory for those who saw mission in terms of the Church offering God to the world, and defeat for those for whom mission was the Church discovering God in the world. Although by no means a unique crisis, it was a powerful symbol because of the inspirational place SIM had held in the international movement, and the central role played by Ted Wickham, then Chairman of the WCC's Advisory Committee on Urban Industrial Mission (see below, pp.96–7).

In Sheffield the Mission shrank drastically. In December 1965 there had been ten members of staff. By September 1966 there were two, Michael Jackson and Andrew Stokes, and Peter Dodd who was working out his notice and who left in the New Year.

Without staff to undertake the work, Jackson stopped most of the remaining industrial mission activity. Much of it had already withered during the prolonged dispute. Conferences and the student summer course were cancelled; Thursday evening Communions were halted, though those who wished to were invited to join the clergy for early morning Communion before their weekly staff meeting. By the end of 1966 Jackson had all but wiped the slate clean.

In industry the response was mixed. Several unions made loud noises in the local press. In Steel, Peech and Tozer, where both Parker and Mackay had been chaplains, a strike on the issue was seriously threatened. In the end the union withdrew all support and the company ceased financial contributions. In one English Steel Corporation plant the union declared that the chaplains were not welcome, but Stokes visited anyway. There was little personal animosity and after a while union opposition crumbled. In some places it was management who were chary of allowing chaplains back into the works fearing that their presence would cause discontent. In fact SIM continued to have access to most companies. The major constraint was the lack of chaplains, not being turned away at the gate.

Amongst the Mission's lay leaders there was an attempt to continue in defiance of the chaplains. The Thursday Evening Group declared itself separate from Jackson, and, with one or two other discussion groups, continued in independent existence. After a little while, however, they all petered out. More people simply voted with their feet, disillusioned with the Church. Some recalled years later that they never again received Holy Communion. That the groups continued at all was a tribute to Wickham's success in establishing a para-church; that they were unsustainable revealed the shallow roots of the enterprise. For some this reflected the laity's "sincerity not being matched by adequate theological understanding";[27] for others it revealed the Church's failure to sustain consistent long term mission – after all, the conversion of Britain had taken several generations.

In industrial mission more widely there were attempts to restate the theological principles on which the movement had been developed, and to offer a critique of Jackson's new-found orthodoxy. The December 1966 issue of *Theology* published a number of articles giving different perspectives on industrial mission. Margaret Kane included a defence of the earlier approach to mission in her unpublished book *Out of Sheffield*. The Methodist Home

Mission Division privately circulated a critique of the Forder Report. But these were small, peripheral voices. The explosion in Sheffield had torn out the heart of the movement. No other team had sufficient authority to unify opposition to Sheffield's change of direction.

Rejection of the past and dissociation of the present mission from its origins dominated the end of 1966 and the beginning of 1967. In an article in *Theology*,[28] Jackson published a vitriolic attack on Wickham, though not by name, on his theology, and on the mission he had created. Industrial mission, Jackson said, had developed its own *syllabus errorum*. It was Gnostic, offering salvation only to those instructed in the true, secret, theology. It was Judaistic, holding the Old Testament as normative and underestimating the person of Jesus. It was Marcionist, proclaiming a God who punishes no-one and who reconciles good and bad indiscriminately. It was Pelagian, asserting that salvation was possible through human efforts. It was pantheist, holding that Christianity was about everyday life, which, said Jackson, it was not. On the contrary, Christianity was about God revealed in Jesus Christ, and only objective theology, and a reaffirmation of salvation by faith alone, could redeem this distorted mission. After 15 years in Wickham's shadow Jackson attacked with the venom and incisiveness of a convert recanting past sins.

More constructively Jackson asserted that "The aims of Industrial Mission do not differ from those of the Christian Church as a whole.".[29] This was a normative prescription for industrial mission and a hope for the future, if somewhat in defiance of its history. Bishop Taylor elaborated the tasks of the Mission as producing a critique of industry, and an understanding of industry in the providence of God.

> "Underlying these tasks is the one basic message which is given to the whole Church to proclaim everywhere. It is the message of God's goodness and love shown to us in Jesus Christ. Christ is the Lord of all life, and, therefore, industry. Mission is, therefore, a task given to the Church. The Church and the apostle are sent by Christ and the message is given and entrusted to them. It is not something they dream up. Problems of mission lie not with the message but with the method, as to how the message is to be said and put into effect. The method problems may be greater in the world of work than in the home or community activity.
>
> "The business of the Church, or any agency of the Church like Industrial Mission, is the making and nurturing of Christians."[30]

The priority of the Church over industry, based on the Lordship of Christ, replaced the acceptance of the secular world, and the people in it, on their own terms. Furthermore Christianity could be applied directly and unambiguously to industrial situations, with no need for "middle axioms" or any mediating device.

In Sheffield the task of reconstruction could commence in earnest with the publication of the Forder report in June 1967. It constituted the foundation document for the new Industrial Mission.

Forder's review of the Mission's attainments damned it with faint praise. The Church, it said, was now listened to in areas where it would previously have met only prejudice and antipathy. However the bridge that the Mission had built had not been used for two-way traffic between industry and the Church. Instead the Mission had become a destination in itself. The authors acknowledged the influence SIM had gained amongst decision takers in industry, yet they implied that the Mission had misused this position, and had aligned the Church with one side, by implication the trades union side, on industrial questions. Furthermore, the Mission had almost wholly neglected the goal of personal conversion. People had not been brought out of industry across the bridge into the Church.

The working party's polite critique continued in their assessment of the impact the Mission had had on the Church. The Church's contact with industry and SIM had, they judged, facilitated the development of an intellectual radicalism, a tendency magnified by the Mission's attractiveness to staff out of sympathy with traditional Church ideas. Consequently the divergence between traditional and radical ideas was at its sharpest in major industrial areas, though they decline to guess at the extent of the Mission's influence on the Church. However they firmly, and by now unnecessarily, rejected the idea of a national Industrial Mission Secretariat.

They also acknowledged that lay support for the Mission was widespread. Yet, they said, SIM had not achieved its aim of developing Christian lay leadership, and had disregarded and by-passed Christian laity already working in industry, to the detriment of its witness.

In sum, they said, the Mission had failed in its aims. Nevertheless, it should continue. The prospects for the renewal and steady development of works visiting were good. Relations with parishes should be strengthened. Ecumenical work should be restored, albeit under the unambiguous authority of the Bishop and Senior Chaplain. Finance should be the exclusive concern of the Church, and donations from industry should be placed in a separate fund. They did not endorse the idea of a Research Institute. New staff should be men of God, faithful in their spiritual vocation, able to communicate their faith to different audiences, mature men with significant experience of ministry. They made a series of recommendations as to the conditions under which chaplains would in future be employed.

But Forder's evaluation of Wickham's Mission was based on preconceptions and assumptions utterly contrary to those which had initiated and guided the Mission. Forder wrote to Hunter to check the accuracy of his summary of the initial aims of the Mission. He characterised these aims as: to build a bridge between Church and industry; to take a step towards the conversion of industrial England; to revitalise the Church by contact with industry; and to gain active lay support and initiative. They were not accurate, Hunter replied. They were wholly misleading. They ignored the utter irrelevance of the Church to industrial society. The Mission's aims had never been articulated in this way and the Mission would not have succeeded if they had been. But Hunter's perspective was too far from that of the Forder enquiry for them to accommodate it. They assumed that the nature of mission was indeed to fish in a muddy pool, and to draw people out of it into the uncontaminated waters of the Church. They could not recognise the Mission's indigenous lay leadership because it was not located in the Churches. Psychologically and theologically they began inside the Church and looked out. Christ, and thus Christian faith, was to be found in the Church.

The Forder enquiry performed the task asked of it and established the basis for a new, orthodox mission firmly anchored in the Anglican Church. Forder proposed new aims for the Mission:

"(a) To win to personal discipleship of Our Lord and to win to the fellowship of His Church those who otherwise would be deprived of Faith in a secular society.

"(b) To present the challenge of the Christian Faith and bring its standards to bear on industrial society.

"(c) To offer Christian pastoral care to workers at all levels."[31]

These became the new guidelines for the development of the Mission. They excluded any consideration of "ministry to the structures", and while there was space for the judgement of industry from a Christian standpoint in its second aim this was to be seen in wholly apolitical terms. No longer was the Mission to concern itself with seeking to influence the culture of industry.

Jackson took the first steps towards the reconstruction of the Mission. Practical, rather than theological or political, concerns were most pressing. The Bishop's Advisory Committee on Industrial Mission was reconvened on an *ad hoc* basis in December 1966 with a new membership and a commitment to drive forward the new Mission. At its first meeting they determined not to repeat what they identified as the mistakes of the past, in particular an antagonism towards parish Churches, and the offering of Christianity in a sugar-coated pill. Chaplains, the Bishop declared, should by-pass the unions, entering works with the approval of the Board alone and appealing directly to the shop-floor worker. He had no time for the careful negotiation of agreement with all parties that had been the foundation stone of the "Sheffield model" of factory visiting.

Finance was critical. In 1965 SIM's income had been just over £7,100, of which 72% had came from industry, including employee giving. Churches and industry also gave support in kind that does not appear in the accounts. This was a powerful argument for involvement by both industrialists and union officials in the Mission's affairs. Donations fell as a consequence of the dispute, but this was matched by the reduction in the Mission's costs with the departure of staff. The diocese also cut its contribution. Bishop Taylor did not want an agency of the Church to be open to such external influence and determined that in future the Church would pay the great bulk of the Mission's costs.

New staff were appointed. In 1967 John Easton and Harry Cole, described as "an older man with fifteen years parish experience",[32] were appointed. So too was Ralph Mayland, in a joint appointment with St Margaret's, Brightside. David Morris came in 1968. A number of experienced parish clergy were recruited as part-time chaplains. A conscious effort was made to ensure that the spread of Anglican churchmanship was represented in these appointments.

Visiting recommenced in a number of factories. By the end of 1967 chaplains were once again visiting English Steel, British Rail, Firth Brown, Hadfields, Edgar Allen, Firth Vickers, Spear and Jackson, and after a gap, Swift Levick. Brown Bayley, British Silver and Samuel Fox became the responsibility of local clergy. Part-time chaplains met monthly with the full-time chaplains, and visited the works under the general oversight of Michael Jackson. There were vacancies at Balfour-Darwin and Sheffield Twist Drill, which had previously had chaplains. Howell Tubes and Stanley Tools wished to begin new chaplaincies. Once again, it was only the lack of staff which constrained the expansion of the Mission.

The new team made strenuous efforts to identify previous supporters and to explain developments to them. Joe Madin, a former Chairman of the Sheffield Trades Council and an active church-goer, was enlisted in their support. On three or four occasions he spoke to groups of trades unionists, bringing his considerable influence to bear on the Mission's behalf. When he died soon after these events SIM raised enough money to establish an annual lecture in his honour. In response to their public relations campaign the chaplains met some opposition and some support, but for most people on the shop-floor and in management the internal conflicts of the Mission were unimportant.

In January 1969 Michael Jackson left the Mission to be incumbent of St George's Church, Doncaster. He had rebuilt SIM from the ruins, but after almost 20 years association with it he cannot have been happy. He had suffered considerable personal antagonism and strain. The Mission he left was smaller, less confident, less adventurous than the one he had taken over. A great deal of pain and harm had been involved in setting a new course. His conception of industrial mission as research had not been realised. The one satisfaction was the feeling that some kind of change had been inevitable, and that he had been right to choose the course that he did. What had once been a heterodox organisation was reconstituted as orthodox and was starting to grow once more.

NOTES

1. Interview with Mr Ken Martin

2. *The Church of God*, F.J.Taylor, 1947

3. Robin Woods, Archdeacon of Sheffield when the new Bishop arrived, said that Taylor came "with a conviction that the mission needed to be sorted out". *An Autobiography*, Robin Woods, SCM Press, 1989, p.129

4. Minute of the Axis meeting of 1.3.60

5. Letter from Mr John Blundell, District Running and Maintenance Engineer, to Mr Ron Hogg, 9.4.62. The phrase "our purpose" presumably refers to the purposes of developing lay leadership, though it could conceivably refer to the purposes of British Railway's management.

6. Minutes of Sheffield Industrial Mission, The Bishop's Committee, 1.2.1960, Item 244

7. "The Tactics and Strategy of Laymen who wish to be effective supporters of the work of the Industrial Mission", unpublished typescript, n/d, [1960/61]

8. Handwritten note, not dated, but from internal evidence some time between April 1961 and March 1962, possibly in preparation for a staff meeting.

9. "Next Steps in Industrial Mission", Michael Jackson, paper given at the Lay Leaders' Residential Conference, 19-20.10.63; also minutes of the Conference and Jackson's handwritten notes.

10. "Major Issues in Industrial Mission", in: *International Review of Missions*, 1965, pp.151-160, emphases in the original

11. "The Sheffield Industrial Mission", Michael Atkinson, in: *Partnership in Ministry*, T. Beeson (ed.), Mowbray, 1964

12 *ibid.*

13. *Systematic Theology* 3 vols., Paul Tillich, James Nisbet & Co., 1964. "First of all, the style, the over-all form, of theonomous works of cultural creation express the ultimacy of meaning even in the most limited vehicles of meaning – a painted flower, a family habit, a technical tool, a form of social intercourse, the vision of a historical figure, an epistemological theory, a political document and so on. None of these things is unconsecrated in a theonomous situation; they are perhaps not consecrated by a church, but they are certainly consecrated in the way they are experienced even without external consecration." Vol. 3, p.266.

Wickham saw theonomy, in the context of the potential relationship between Church and society, as a magnificent but questionable condition. The structures and constitution of the Church of England, he said, assume the condition of theonomy as the ideal norm, but the danger, into which the Church had fallen, was a descent into mere conformity and into an "ideological superstructure". *Church and People in an Industrial Society*, E.R. Wickham, Lutterworth Press, 1957, p.229. Tillich is reputed to have commented on a visit to Sheffield, that "this is the only place in the world where my theology is being put into effect".

14. "Christian Mission in Industry", M.J. Jackson (ed.), 1964, unpublished.

15. In 1967 the Sheffield Council of Churches published a survey of church-goers. Of the 860 people they surveyed only 11 participated in industrial mission, of whom one was retired, and one not in industry. The author, Martin Reardon, estimated that when it was fully staffed the Mission had been in touch with 15-20% of the population of Sheffield. He judged that this discrepancy probably reflected a mixture of reasons: that few church goers-worked in industry; that of those that did few participated actively in the Mission; or that few Industrial Mission people participated in the survey.

16. *Honest to God*, John Robinson, SCM, 1963, p.25. Robinson describes Wickham, with Dr George Macleod, as the two men "who are as exercised as any in our generation by the relation of theology to the real world", p.11

17. *The Secular Meaning of the Gospel*, Paul van Buren, SCM, 1963, p. xiv

18. Robinson came to a SIM Conference straight from the trial, with a newspaper which reported his words under his arm. Archbishop Fisher publicly censured him for his stance. Secular theology was accompanied by what was called "the New Morality" which, in its critics' view, legitimated any action which could be justified by love. The key book in this movement was *Situation Ethics*, Joseph Fletcher, SCM, 1966.

19. A more detailed, though still partial, account is told in "The Origins, Context and Ideology of Industrial Mission 1875-1975", E.H. Lurkins, unpublished PhD thesis, London School of Economics, 1981, pp.227-90. The whole affair grew confused and there is little profit in detailing events blow by blow.

20. "Sheffield due for Relegation", Revd Alan Patient, *New Christian*, 18.11.65; reprinted in *The Sheffield Star*, 19.11.65.
    Parker had contacts with both the *New Christian* and *The Times*; Geoffrey Moorhouse of *The Guardian* spent some time in Sheffield interviewing people. Many local people had good links with *The Sheffield Star* and *The Sheffield Morning Telegraph*.

21. *The Times*, 21.6.66; *The Guardian*, 23.7.66

22. Letter from Bishop Taylor to Mr. A.D.Clegg, English Steel Corporation Management Group, 23.12.65

23. *The Future of the Sheffield Industrial Mission*, A Report by a Working Party, May 1967, [in fact published in June 1967]

24. "Sheffield Industrial Mission", Report to the Bishop of Sheffield, E. Barker, S.F.Linsley, T.Chapman, July 1966, pp.18-19

25. Reprinted in full in *New Christian*, 28.7.66

26. *ibid.*

27. *The Future of the Sheffield Industrial Mission*, A Report by a Working Party, May 1967, p.9

28. "No New Gospel", Michael Jackson, *Theology*, Vol. LXIX, No. 558, December 1966, pp.539-544

29. *ibid.*, p.539

30. "The Essential Message of SIM", Bishop Taylor, Minutes of the Directors' Group, 14.11.67

31. *The Future of the Sheffield Industrial Mission*, A Report by a Working Party, May 1967, p.11

32. Minutes of the *ad hoc* Bishop's Advisory Committee on Industrial Mission, 17.2.67

4

THE RESTORATION OF CONFIDENCE, 1969-1974

1969-1974, Reconstruction

On Michael Jackson's departure, Andrew Stokes became Senior Chaplain. There was a great deal to be done.

Stokes set his hand to the long term goals of re-establishing the Mission's reputation, and of restoring confidence. He was not particularly interested in doing battle with the Mission's past. He looked forward, working with the team to develop an understanding of mission that was deep rooted in orthodox Christian faith and practice.

A number of events enabled Stokes to work without the sense of continuing conflict. In April 1970 Bishop Taylor had a second stroke which further debilitated him and led to his retirement 12 months later. His successor was William Gordon Fallows, an altogether more emollient man. Stokes had been his pupil at Ripon Hall 10 years earlier and they had remained friends. In 1967 the partial nationalisation of the steel industry was followed by considerable reorganisation in the largest works in Sheffield. Many people moved jobs and firms and many of the old union networks were disrupted. Steel, Peech and Tozer, for example, was merged with Parkgate Iron and Steel to become part of the British Steel Corporation. The passing of time helped memories fade and wounds heal.

The early 1970s was also a period of considerable social and economic volatility. The steel industry had been accustomed to a rapid roller-coaster ride of boom-and-bust. In 1971 many workers were on short-time. The next year business lurched upwards, and they were suddenly working long hours of overtime. Nationally, the political economy was in crisis. The Conservative government under Edward Heath was in conflict with the unions. Oil prices rocketed after the Egypt-Israel war in October 1973, sending shock waves through the economy. In 1974 a second clash with the miners in two years led to the three-day week and a general election. In South Yorkshire mining, heavy industry and union strength meant that national events were felt close to home.

Against this background the Mission again began to grow. In 1969 five full-time and eight part-time staff had visited 20 companies. By 1971, with one more full-time member of staff, 30 firms were visited. However, staff recruited in 1967 left together in 1972 at the end of their five-year contracts, and Stokes was left carrying the Mission's work with part-time colleagues and just two chaplains appointed that year, Malcolm Grundy and John Thompson, who worked three days a week for the Mission and three days with St Margaret's, Brightside. The departing chaplains all moved to parochial appointments. Ralph Mayland continued as a part-time member of staff.

The first pillar of SIM's renewed confidence lay in a return to the undramatic daily routine of works visiting and pastoral care. The flavour of the Mission had changed. Chaplains put more weight on biblical and doctrinal teaching, and though they would tackle topical issues these were not allowed to edge out explicitly Christian foci. Chaplains were perceived to be more "churchy", more like vicars than their predecessors, more outsiders. They were meticulous about retaining a political independence, and, perhaps as a consequence, the Mission was thought to have lost some of its earlier emphasis on social justice, and affinity with the shop-floor worker.

In Stocksbridge, for example, the firm of Samuel Fox & Co. had been visited regularly by Ted Wickham from 1948, and, apart from a brief hiatus in 1966, visiting had continued steadily since then. In the 1950s SIM had created an extensive network of lay leaders through many of the firms' departments. This collapsed in 1964 and was replaced by a small advisory committee, chaired for several years by the chairman of the Works Consultative Committee, Mr K.C.P. Wattsford. Industrial Mission had enjoyed consistent support from the senior management of the firm. In 1968 it became part of the Alloy and Stainless Steel Division of BSC.

Fox's was a large works which drew a very high proportion of its work force from the village of Stocksbridge. It thus had an apparently natural link with the parish Church. Yet visiting had largely been undertaken by full-time chaplains with some support from local clergy. From 1967 Jackson sought to change the balance with parochial clergy responsible for the bulk of visiting, supported by a full-time chaplain, Andrew Stokes. The team comprised the new incumbent of Stocksbridge, B.H. (Peter) Hawkins (who had previously worked in Detroit where he knew the Industrial Mission and its leader Hugh White), his curates, Maurice Friggens and Tim Leach, and Ian Harland, then vicar at Oughtibridge and later Bishop of Carlisle. For a period half of the Mission's part-time chaplains were visiting this one firm.

Chaplains concentrated on regular visiting and pastoral care. Some workers attended the "Trades Unions in Society" Conference in 1970, and there were occasional services in St Matthias' Church to which workers were invited. Lunch-time discussion meetings were held each Lent. In 1969 and 1970 these took place in the parish church. In 1971, perhaps indicating a greater confidence, meetings were held in the works' conference room. They were "aimed at improving human relations at work", reflecting Stokes' perception that relations in the works were poor.[1]

Yet, despite the major commitment of the Mission to this works, there was still cause for concern. Significant areas of the works were not visited, and even where visiting was regular chaplains often found it difficult to talk to the workers because of the nature of their jobs. Donations were in decline. Despite the turmoil in the Mission individual giving by the work force had continued. In 1968 donations had averaged around £10 per week. By April 1971 they were down to around £5. The absence of a full-time chaplain was one reason offered for the fall. On the departure of Maurice Friggens at the end of 1970 the Bishop agreed to appoint a full-time chaplain, who would also undertake Sunday duties at St Matthias'. Incumbent and curates would continue to visit. Ironically, but in good faith, this return to the previous pattern was announced as an experiment designed to strengthen the link between the works and the parish.

Chaplains also explored ways in which they might work better with lay Christians in the works. In 1967 Stokes had identified four weaknesses. Lay Christians were often isolated from one another and unaware of who else in the works was a Christian. To be effective, industrial mission should create a truly lay mission, while avoiding the trap of developing lay leadership uncommitted to the Church. At the same time industrial mission needed to be embedded in the work of the whole Church, and to build up some sense of the body of Christ in an industrial context. Underlying these concerns was the belief that to tackle these weaknesses was to engender effective evangelism, and thus to bring people into the Churches.

One experiment was a group of managers in the English Steel Corporation, convened by Andrew Stokes. This was first called the "Committed Christians" group, a title rapidly replaced by the anodyne "First Tuesday of the Month". It aspired, at least in Stokes' eyes, to be "the Church in ESC". In contrast to a para-church this group was to be the Church in the sense that Christian lay people expressed their faith together at their place of work. It most closely resembled a traditional Christian Union meeting. Criteria for membership of the group included membership of a denominational Church, and a commitment to aim to attend Church regularly, to read the Bible and pray daily, and that members should offer themselves as "tools of Christ". Associate membership was available to any who could not meet all these criteria. The group met monthly each winter between December 1966 and May 1972. Most time was spent in discussing overtly religious topics, for example, prayer, the Church, the Holy Spirit, miracles.

From 1970 the group took religious and secular topics in turn: a series on Jesus' "I am" sayings was interleaved with sessions on aspects of the criminal law. Membership was never large: the circulation list did not exceed 15 people, and attendance, once a month through the winter, was no more than ten.

Stokes convened a similar group with people drawn from a variety of firms across Sheffield. It was called "Christians at Work" and ran from 1971 to 1974. Its motivation was the conviction that occasional visits by clergy could not be the whole of industrial mission. The effective work of mission in industry had to be undertaken by church-going, Christian laity who were there all their working lives. By contrast with Wickham's teaching that anyone could do God's work, whether or not they were Christian, Stokes argued that Christian work could only be done by Christian people.

Group members agreed to pray for one other and for their work, to study the bearing of faith on work, to press for the inclusion of work in all aspects of worship in local Churches, and to become a real Christian presence in industry and commerce. The group met monthly and held residential conferences together, but its membership never exceeded 30, and in 1974 Stokes closed it down. The intention that the group be controlled by its lay membership had not been achieved. Like many such groups it had achieved a nucleus of committed members which had then become a congenial club. It had failed in its aim of inspiring its members to express their faith more actively at work and thus to further the mission of the Church.

Grundy's appointment in Rotherham in 1972 had particular sensitivities. Work in the area had previously been dominated by Steel, Peech and Tozer which remained hostile to SIM. In 1967 it had been felt prudent to withdraw from the area altogether and to sell the house the Mission owned there. Grundy drew on his experience before ordination and blended detached youth work techniques with training skills and works visiting to develop a ministry to the community of Rotherham as a whole. He visited Parkgate Rolling Mills, part of British Steel, going round the shop floor and offices on a regular basis, careful to arrive for lunch at the different canteens on a regular pattern. He expanded work with apprentices that John Easton had begun, and was given space on management training courses at British Steel's training centre, Brookfield Manor. He became chaplain to the Retired Employees Association in Rotherham, was an active member of the Junior Chamber of Commerce, and built links with a wide range of local organisations. In so doing he built up a ministry focused on helping people to reflect on the social and moral aspects of their work. He was able to get alongside some of those deeply involved in the economic and political turmoil of the time, offering support, critical observations, and pastoral care where it was needed to those in work and out.

Alongside visiting, the second pillar of SIM's restoration of confidence was the consolidation of a secure organisation. Bishop Taylor's *ad hoc* Advisory Committee was formalised in November 1968. Both trades unions and management were represented, as they had been in the past. However, although the Senior Chaplain attended the meeting, sometimes with colleagues, chaplains were no longer full members. In 1968 SIM felt sufficiently confident to hold a public Annual General Meeting, the first since 1965, though the meeting would have no role in setting policy for the Mission. Finance remained important, but Taylor's determination to pay the full costs of the Mission was not sustained. In the early 1970s approximately half of the Mission's recorded income was from the Church, and half from industry (both company and individual giving). Each year a small loss or surplus was recorded, and the Mission was investing in property.

Ecumenical relations were sore, but not irreparable, although the Mission remained firmly Anglican. The Committee was dominated by the Bishop, the Archdeacon of Sheffield, and Anglican preoccupations. Nevertheless by 1972 it welcomed a member from the Methodist Church, and another from the United Reform Church in 1973. Free Church part-time chaplains were encouraged. In September 1968 a Salvationist, H. Colin McAuley, began a chaplaincy in Dunford Hadfield's, and a Methodist, John Williams, had joined the team by 1971. The Roman Catholic Bishop of Hallam, Gerald Moverley, was approached. Although he expressed interest in a Catholic priest becoming a chaplain no name was put forward.

Sheffield Industrial Mission was still largely excluded from national industrial mission developments, partly by its own choice, and partly by the antipathy of industrial chaplains elsewhere. The new staff at Sheffield were divided on the value of the Industrial Mission Association, and decided against involvement. However Stokes continued to participate, though it could be personally uncomfortable, and in 1969 he and Charles Grice were elected to the IMA executive. When Grundy was appointed in 1972 he visited all the larger missions around the country as part of his own induction into industrial mission work; it also helped break the ice between SIM and other teams.

On the twin pillars of works visiting and organisational soundness other activities could also recommence. An occasional conferences was held. In 1967 a conference on worship had been poorly attended. In 1970 a conference was held on the theme of "Trades Unions in Society" which was well received by those who attended, but a second was cancelled for lack of interest.

The Mission began training theological students once more. Stokes visited a number of colleges and arranged training tailored to particular groups. Two or three students, including Raymond Draper, came for a few months to work in industry and receive guided reading from Andrew Stokes. The summer course for ordinands was relaunched in 1969.

A number of groups were drawn together from across the region. The Directors' Group reflected Forder's concern that the Mission should continue to address those who were powerful in industry. It met monthly each winter from 1966 to 1979, by which time most of its members had become retired or redundant directors. At each meeting a talk would be followed by discussion. The first two speakers were the Provost of Sheffield and Bishop Taylor. The programme was leavened with the occasional dinner.

Relations with parishes were consistently reported to be improving, but this is impossible to assess. The appointment of Ralph Mayland, half-time industrial chaplain and half-time incumbent, was in part to try to bridge the gap. His attempts to bring industrial issues into the worship at St Margaret's were met by incomprehension or the resentment of parishioners. He also found coping with industrial mission, the congregation, and a new housing estate physically gruelling. John Thompson, who took over from Mayland in 1972, found the link between industrial mission and parochial concerns largely implicit. Industrial mission was "just something the vicar did". However, when Thompson moved to St Silas, Broomhall, the congregation were less accommodating. They regarded industrial mission work as a distraction from his real work in the parish.

Stokes put a great deal of energy into consolidating links between the Mission and the parishes. He introduced the "Study Day" to introduce clergy and ministers to industry and to the working conditions experienced by some of their congregation. They visited a works and talked with some of the employees. By and large he succeeded in building up the confidence of the parochial clergy in the Mission. Yet it was always difficult to go beyond this relationship. The Mission was unable to persuade clergy to integrate industrial issues into their worship and teaching, or to inspire the laity to more effective Christian witness at work through parish-based activity. The disjunction between local Church life and the Mission's sphere of activity remained.

Apart from the innovation of the Study Day, the new Mission picked up the techniques of the old. In large part this was because the Mission inherited its predecessor's access to the works and the workers' expectations of it, though part of its motivation may also have been to show that previous successes could be repeated on different principles. One aspect of the old approach was conspicuously not repeated. The new Mission eschewed any hint of "ministry to the structures". Instead Stokes felt that if Christian influence was to be brought to bear on events it would be through personal contacts, talking, sometimes critically, supporting and praying for people with power and with those who faced difficult decisions.

1969 was the 25th anniversary of the Mission's foundation. It was celebrated with an exhibition in the Cathedral and publicity in parish magazines, works' papers, and other local publications. Two receptions were held, one for clergy and the other for members of industry. The tone of the publicity was perhaps a little tentative. Industrial Mission was described as growing, but still experimental, still seeking new ways of proclaiming the gospel in the modern industrial world.

The spirituality of the new, experimental Mission remained securely based in conventional Church life, both orthodox and catholic. To both industrial and ecclesiastical audiences chaplains were described as parish priests located in factories. The aim of mission was to bring individuals to Christian faith, and into Church membership. This was largely expressed and discussed in conventional Christian language. Where chaplains had to translate Christian ideas into the vernacular, because people were unfamiliar with theological terms, the intention was always to find a way to communicate a conventional Christian understanding. Translation was not, as with secular theology, a component of adapting Christianity to modern conditions. It was entirely acceptable to discuss secular issues, and matters of social concern in the works, but the focus remained the proclamation of the Gospel.

The quality of mission was grounded in each chaplain's own devotional life. David Morris outlined the typical day of a chaplain:[2]

Early morning worship

Deal with correspondence

Works visiting in several departments

Lunch (often working)

Possibly attend meetings on the shop-floor or in the offices

Visit other departments in the works, or possibly someone in hospital

Evening meeting

Evensong

Preparation for the next day

Harry Cole visiting Spear and Jackson, 1969.

The Provost of Sheffield Cathedral, The Very Revd Frank Curtis, Mrs Fanny Mudia and the Rt Revd James Mudia, Bishop of Maseno North, Kenya, visiting a steel works with Malcolm Grundy.

One of the highlights of the annual Theological Students' course is an underground pit visit, here at Houghton Main in July, 1992.

The IMSY staff in 1994. (left to right) John Kenward, Roy Newell, Norman Young, Barry Parker, Elizabeth Nash, Margaret Halsey, Mike West, Tony Attwood, Chris Sissons.

The chaplain was to be an accessible priest, freed from the burdens of parochial administration. He was to seek the truth, to live in co-operation with others, and to help where he could. This impelled him to speak out, to question and to teach, though this did not imply political activity. He was also to share the Christian faith in the hope that others would come to know its value.

Stokes' emphasis was on work with individuals. The implications of Christian faith were worked out through the lives of Christian believers, not least through their working life. The example and pattern of Jesus' life, and in particular the self-denial and sacrifice shown in his birth in a stable and death on a cross, were the model for everyone. To follow Jesus was to embrace his humility, weakness, and selflessness. Strength, wealth, and power were not proper goals of the Christian life. Where they existed they were to be used for the benefit of others.

Writing much later Stokes elaborated the idea of following the example of Christ, stressing the role of the chaplain as a sacrificial sign. He thought that some Mission activities, such as convening study groups in the corners of people's working lives, or becoming expert on industrial relations or management theory, though valuable, were not sufficient; and diving into militant unionism was a denial of the Gospel of reconciliation. Instead,

"I would often ask myself what I was doing there [in the works]. I had no church buildings to care for, no services to prepare, no church council to meet, only rarely someone to marry or bury... I stood in dark workshops on summer days, got my suit sprayed with cooling fluid from machine tools, let sparks from the furnaces burn holes in my clerical shirt, and shouted into people's ears as we tried to talk to each other. I shared bitter stewed tea out of people's billy cans and sometimes an exalted glass of gin, and listened to their anxieties and their anger. Whatever was I doing there? All I seemed to be able to do was to take bits of it home and offer them to God in rather confused prayer.

"I concluded eventually that, whatever else I might do in the way of teaching or pastoral care, there was only one fundamental reason for being there. I was a sign. To all those thousands of people, my presence was meant to say 'God our Father knows that you are here, he knows what it is like, and he will not let you go'... He sits with us by the waters of Babylon and we weep together. We are not as alienated as we thought."[3]

Despite the Mission's individualist focus, political debate was not absent. The Bishop's Advisory Committee, for example, had a heated discussion over the merits or otherwise of proposed industrial relations legislation. Stokes spoke out against the immorality of the asset-stripping done to Jessop Saville. But, despite the economic and political turbulence of the times, it was not SIM's place as a Church organisation to publicly involve itself in political issues. For example, in the summer of 1971 there was a proposal to move River Don Stampings out of BSC and into Firth Brown's, and to close the heavy forgings and casting sections. With Stokes, the chaplains at the works, Harry Cole, Ted Longman, and David Morris, wrote to *The Times* opposing the closure and loss of employment. They thus supported the trades unions' campaign, and also the position taken privately by local management. The transfer was called off. Yet Stokes found it necessary to defend his letter both in the local paper, saying that SIM was concerned about jobs, not the merits of the proposed transfer, and also to the SIM Advisory Committee which was divided over the wisdom and content of their public stance.

When he did express a public concern for social justice, Stokes tended to recast political categories into a moral framework. In his 1972 annual report he focused on the moral consequences of developments in industrial relations, and in 1974, he wrote,

"I believe that industrial society faces a growing moral crisis, of which the foci are liberty, greed, urbanism, and leadership."[4]

Chaplains could not evade the issues of injustice and turmoil which they faced daily in their visits and meetings. Moral and political concerns are very close, and it may have been both more natural and more acceptable to express concerns about public policy in moral rather than political terms.

When Andrew Stokes left the Mission in 1974 he had attained his central objectives. Internal confidence had been restored. New staff had been appointed and the spread of the Mission's work extended. It had been successfully rebuilt on an entirely orthodox and catholic basis. Chaplains were welcome in industry, and Sheffield Industrial Mission had become an acceptable part of life in the Churches.

1975-1979, The Culture of Industry

At the end of 1974 Malcolm Grundy took over from Andrew Stokes. He had come into industrial mission less by design than by the opportunities open to him as curate at St George's Church, Doncaster. There he had taken over some of Charles Grice's work with apprentices at Markham Main (see below, Chapter 6), and had reopened a chaplaincy at the railway plant works. This had fallen into abeyance, having previously been undertaken by Gerald Hollis, though it had always been separate from SIM. In 1972, at the end of his curacy, Andrew Stokes approached him with an invitation to join the Mission team.

Grundy's succession was not automatic. He was first appointed as Acting Senior Chaplain, and then, somewhat to his surprise, was asked by Bishop Fallows to become Senior Chaplain. In Church terms he was relatively inexperienced, though he could draw on previous experience in youth work and work with voluntary and community groups. He inherited a team solidly grounded in works visiting and with sufficient confidence to expand into new areas of work.

There was a great deal of continuity between Stokes's leadership and Grundy's. Grundy's priorities were to build up the team and to continue the process of re-establishing the Mission. He also wished to address some of the larger issues of industrial culture and the changes associated with new technology, in particular the rapidly growing threat of unemployment. This took the Mission into new ways of working. Significantly, Grundy discovered the Forder report in the Mission's files. It had become a document of historical interest and no longer a guide for the Mission's development.

The number of chaplains grew rapidly. In 1975 there were five full- and half-time chaplains, and seven part-time chaplains. By the end of 1979 there were seven full- and half-time chaplains, and 16 part-timers. Stokes had worked hard to mend fences between the SIM and other denominations, but it was not until Grundy's arrival that relationships were fully restored. In large part this was possible because no longer did anyone in the team have any personal connection with the troubles of the mid-1960s. Gordon Wilson, a Methodist, was appointed full-time in 1974, after careful and detailed negotiations about his contract of employment. In January 1979 a United Reformed Church minister, Elizabeth Nash, was appointed half-time. It had been over 12 years since the team had included a woman. In 1980 Mike Kelly became the first Roman Catholic priest to be appointed as a part-time chaplain.

The team continued to meet weekly at 7.30am on a Monday morning for Holy Communion, followed by breakfast, bible study, prayer and business. Once a month they were joined by the part-time staff. Most of the team shared a broad evangelical outlook, motivated both by a desire to present the Gospel in the works, and also by a broader concern to apply the Gospel to society.

Works visiting continued as the foundation of all the Mission's activities. The growth in the number of chaplains enabled works visiting both to expand and to diversify, though it remained concentrated in steel and heavy engineering. In 1974 John Thompson became chaplain to sweet manufacturers George Bassett Holdings. It was seen as a new departure; the mission had lost all memory of Kay Hancock's visits to the firm in the 1950s. In 1974 also an approach was made to the cutlery manufacturers, Viners, and although the proposal fell through at this stage a chaplaincy was started in 1980. The first chaplaincies outside manufacturing, in the large retail stores Debenhams and Sainsbury's, were undertaken by Elizabeth Nash who also had responsibility for work on unemployment. (Staff at Sheffield Cathedral and the URC Central Mission had well established chaplaincies in four large stores in the centre of the city, but these were not part of SIM.) Industrial mission in the coalfields was recommenced under David Lawrance, and John Smith became the first full time chaplain to visit Brown Bayleys since 1966.

Chaplains continued to run discussion groups for the Christian laity, and a few long running discussion groups continued in certain works. Outside work, one group met regularly in the Wortley Arms, and another, the "Topic Group", met monthly each winter. This group was attended by around 30 managers and had speakers of national reputation from both Church and industry. The "Directors Group" met at Grundy's home conveniently following the regular meeting of the Engineering Employers' Federation. It proved to be a useful route in introducing SIM to new companies.

John Thompson nurtured a different type of group in Bassetts. With the support of the Managing Director, Bill Mills, he drew together a group focused on contemplative spirituality called the Society of Brother Lawrence. Lawrence was a 17th-century French monk who wrote that through "the practice of the real presence of God" he was as much at prayer in the noise and clutter of the monastery kitchen as in saying the hours. Thompson applied this to the works. Adult spiritual life, he said, was always lived in the presence of God, no matter what else the disciple was doing. He contrasted this approach with the superficial activism and this-worldly involvement which he felt characterised much of the contemporary Church under the influence of John Robinson and secular theology. Bill Mills arranged for the printing of a small card which quoted Brother Lawrence's words and these were liberally distributed. At most around nine or ten people came to the group. They were not the women who were the majority of the work force at Bassetts, but departmental managers and others of similar grade. Partly because of constant staff movement, the group proved impossible to sustain.

Geographically Grundy sought to spread the mission more effectively across the Diocese. Most chaplains were based in Sheffield, but, apart from 1967-1972, at least one had lived in Rotherham in order to identify better with the Borough. When Grundy became Senior Chaplain he moved from Rotherham to Sheffield, and it was some time before Raymond Draper was appointed to replace him there. Grundy also wanted to reinforce SIM's presence in Doncaster. Here industrial mission work had historically proceeded parallel with SIM, but administratively separate from it. The Coalfields Chaplain, David Lawrance, lived in Doncaster and was given the responsibility of overseeing the development of other chaplaincies in that part of the Diocese, but it was slow work.

Work also continued with local Churches. Chaplains took part in training sessions with congregations, and a study day for local clergy and ministers was held each April. The summer student course continued with an average of 25 students a year. Students on longer term placements were infrequent, and most came from overseas, in particular from West Africa and India.

SIM was also now in a position to restore relations with the national industrial mission movement. In 1975, for the first time, all full-time chaplains attended the Industrial Mission Association national conference.

Alongside the continuity of works visiting, Grundy brought several new elements to SIM. The Church, he asserted, was not concerned with the mechanics of industry, but with its underlying culture, its goals and organisation. Christian interests lay in promoting industry that was just and participatory, and in contributing to a more humane and responsible society which acknowledged the dignity of each person. The role of the chaplain was to express the Church's concern through pastoral care, and to encourage individual Christians and others of goodwill to participate more fully in policy making. Chaplains identified themselves with people in industry in their struggle towards a greater humanity, but they also kept sufficient independence to be able to raise questions around the values and principles by which people lived their lives. Grundy was described as a "cuckoo in the nest"[5] in following this balancing act. Training proved to be an ideal context for instigating these discussions of value and purpose. In the Church, the chaplains' role was to educate clergy into the realities of people's working lives and to evoke a well informed and sympathetic understanding of industry. Such knowledge was seen as a precondition of the Church's ability to address industry effectively.

Grundy very largely accepted both the Church and industry on their own terms. He affirmed what each was doing, and he sought to use the Mission to help them do it better.

Industrial participation was seen as a key element in encouraging industry to move in the direction of giving greater respect and dignity to its work force. It was also a theme to which chaplains could actively contribute. Chaplains attended many works councils which were official forums for discussion of most aspects of the life of a works. They attended as observers and sometimes as participants. When the Bullock Report on Industrial Democracy[6] was published chaplains endorsed its recommendations and organised discussion groups to promote its message and to explore its implications. Private firms tended to lag behind, but BSC was actively discussing the possibility of Worker Directors. The movement was destroyed after the 1979 election.

Grundy was also concerned to address the way industry was changing. He was a member of the Technology Frontier Group, established by the Sheffield Regional Centre for Science and Technology, part of Sheffield City Polytechnic. This was an informal "think tank" of people from industry and education who could evaluate new technology, in an attempt to identify what new industries would grow in the area, and to assess the educational implications of such changes.

He was helped to raise these issues in the Churches by a national initiative. In 1975 the Archbishop of Canterbury, Donald Coggan, sought to encourage a debate through the Churches on the kind of society that was generally wanted, and the kind of people necessary to achieve it. There was a new sense in the Church that such concerns, though large scale and difficult to grasp, were nevertheless a proper concern of the Church at large.

To promote debate in the Churches SIM produced a booklet entitled *The Church and Industrial Society*.[7] John Habgood, then Bishop of Durham, wrote on "The Christian Viewpoint" arguing that part of the human task was to use the natural world for the glory of God. Technology should be appreciated, but it should be used for the benefit of all. Grundy looked at paradoxical attitudes to work as both a curse and a blessing, and he warned of the need to respond constructively to impending mass unemployment. A layman, Michael Grylls, had at SIM's invitation attended a hearing on the merits or otherwise of the fast breeder nuclear reactor convened by the British Council of Churches, and he summarised the issues for the booklet. The final essay was contributed by Julian Lessey of the Conservation Society on the theme of "The End of Economic Growth – What Next?".

This was one of a small number of publications aimed primarily at clergy, and all designed to promote debate on industrial or social issues. A booklet on Work was produced in connection with a debate in Diocesan Synod in October 1978 on the crisis in employment. An information sheet was produced on closed shop trades union agreements to coincide with a General Synod Debate on the issue. The largest part of these publications gave factual information on the topic. Explicitly Christian content was slight, or was expounded in a section separate from the substance of the issue. The implication of this methodology was that neither the nature of the Christian mission nor the Christian message were at all problematic, except that better informed Christians would be better equipped to respond to the issues.

A further spur to the chaplains' discussion of the changing culture of industry was provided by the British Council of Churches and Christian Aid in 1977. The chaplains as a team agreed to participate in the "Britain Today and Tomorrow" study project, despite the short time scale, in part because "from the many different areas within the Church, we have heard generalisations and false assumptions about life in industry".[8] Chaplains surveyed the attitudes and opinions of 100 people at different levels in the steel industry. They found that many companies had problems of morale and industrial relations. An underlying theme was the long-term trend towards ever lower employment levels, which held worrying implications for long-term unemployment. There was, however, little concern about the supply of raw materials, but rather an overwhelming confidence in the potential of technology for materials substitution. Most respondents thought industry should have a conscience, but this immediately died the death of a thousand qualifications. No thought was given in industry to the moral dimensions of economic growth. Industrial participation was met with ambivalence and hostility. When asked what they understood by "economic justice", a phrase much used by the original BCC document, most answered in terms of industrial relations, and these were not good. Ominously the chaplains recorded that "never, or perhaps not until the present day, has there been a feeling that the industry is in decline".[9]

The survey revealed a great deal about the standing of the chaplains in the steel industry. At the start of the project they had expressed anxiety as to how their questions would be received by an industry which did not take kindly to criticism. Their success in administering the questionnaire indicated a renewed and mutual confidence in their relationship with industry. They also rediscovered the thoughtfulness of many of industry's managers, but they failed to use the survey's own evidence on the dire condition of ethical discussion in the industry. They concluded that, for Christian ministry to be effective, clergy should have a greater understanding of, and sympathy for, industry, and if industrial and urban values were wrong then Christians must push much harder to influence those places where attitudes were formed.

"In Universities, in research establishments, in industry, men still look for a moral base for their actions. Our Christian faith can offer this, and so much more, if only as Churches we can listen more sensitively to the questions which are being asked."[10]

This was an inadequate prescription. The chaplains had discovered that the values they held dear, including moral decision making in industry, and industrial participation, were not widely endorsed or popular. This raised the question of the true nature of the relationship that the Church's mission had with an industry which was at best amoral, or with good people in an amoral industry. It suggested that the ability of the Mission to effect change in industry was minimal. But these issues were not addressed at the time.

Their report also observed in passing that some of the terminology used in the BCC questionnaire meant nothing to those interviewed in the steel works. But this was now a practical, not a theological, point: if the Church wished to influence industry, they said, it should speak in a language which industry understood.

Of all the salient issues of the 1970s the one that threatened to overwhelm those concerned for the wellbeing of society was the sharp growth in unemployment. In the mid 1970s youth unemployment began to rise alarmingly, and South Yorkshire was hard hit. As the decade progressed there was equal concern for the number of workers made redundant, and wider fears for a society characterised by long-term mass unemployment.

The response to unemployment reshaped industrial mission. SIM became identified as the local Church agency knowledgable about unemployment, and actively concerned to respond to it. SIM distributed a paper designed to help clergy counsel those experiencing redundancy. It provided factual information to promote debate in the Churches, and chaplains preached and spoke about the evil of unemployment and the potential of the Churches to respond. Grundy had good links with local authority youth and careers services and with voluntary agencies responding to unemployment. In May 1976, jointly with the Church and Industry Committee of the Sheffield District of the Methodist Church, SIM convened a consultation on youth unemployment addressed by Harold Walker MP, then Minister of State at the Department of Employment. In 1979 Elizabeth Nash was appointed in part to address unemployment. Grundy unsuccessfully entered into negotiations to establish a chaplaincy to the Manpower Services Commission (MSC), a government agency concerned with unemployment, whose headquarters were relocated to Sheffield at the end of the 1970s.

But information and intellectual debate were insufficient, and by definition unemployment was not amenable to works visiting. SIM began to be increasingly involved in practical action. In 1977, with help from a Nigerian student on a placement organised by the Church Missionary Society, SIM acted as "sponsor" for six young people undergoing work experience in a variety of Church linked places of employment. At the same time Grundy was working on other schemes. He negotiated with a variety of agencies to appoint an unemployment counsellor in the Dearne Valley, an area of South Yorkshire with very high unemployment. He encouraged Attercliffe parish to set up a tapestry and sewing workshop. Neither initiative succeeded.

"Workshop 6" did succeed. Grundy convened a small group of people who wished to set up a practical project for unemployed young people. They commissioned a study which identified two gaps in local industry such a project might address, repairing supermarket trolleys, and a foundry for small tonnages of metal. The group chose the latter. They negotiated with the MSC for funds, convincing the civil servants that they could set up the project as a group of individuals and that they did not need to function under the banner of SIM, or the Church, or any other organisation. After two years' preparation the project was off the ground and, after a further 18 months doing up the cavernous workshop, they were in business smelting aluminium. Grundy was Company Secretary.

The process by which SIM moved from concern, through information provision and into practical action was not the outworking of a conscious strategy. Like Topsy, it just grew. As a consequence neither the practical nor the theological implications for the Mission were properly debated or evaluated until the 1980s.

Approval for the Mission's concern with industrial culture was not universal. One of the members of the Director's Group wrote that he looked to the Mission for its unique contribution, but

> "increasingly what I was getting from the Mission (and from the Church) was amateur politics and amateur economics; the Mission's efforts should not, I submit, be put at the service of fashionable propositions, political or economic, which they are not, to say the least, sufficiently well placed to understand or judge."[11]

But Grundy was in tune with much of the Church. Industrial mission was operating in a political sphere, but it did so in a way that was congenial to the majority of clergy. There was a widespread feeling that unemployment was wrong, and that something must be done. Practical responses, and in particular ameliorative schemes initiated by Churches and funded through the MSC, were widely seen as acceptable and appropriate. There was little critical analysis of the causes of unemployment, nor vocal political campaigning. The Church could be seen to take action, without causing offence.

In 1979 SIM was again facing internal change. In August 1979 Bishop Fallows died. He had worked closely with both Stokes and Grundy, and had encouraged his senior staff to take an active role in supporting the Mission. He had reinforced its ecumenical progress. The Mission again played a full part in the national industrial mission movement. It had the confidence of both industry and the Churches, and the chaplains had found a new assurance in their dealings with industry. The Mission was at a stage when decisions would have to be made about its future direction and structure. However Grundy was due to leave at the end of the year, and discussion was held in abeyance until the new Bishop and new Senior Chaplain were appointed.

Nationally too there were ominous changes. The Winter of Discontent had been followed by the arrival of Margaret Thatcher at the head of a radical Conservative government. Her election marked the end of consensus politics which had made possible the Mission's place in industry. The impact of an abrupt change of attitude towards industry was felt quickly and very close to home.

1980-1981, Steel strike

The first national steel strike since 1926 was a dangerous time for industrial mission. The strike arose from British Steel's determination to cut one third of its work force, 52,000 workers nationally, and to offer only a small wage increase to those that remained. The unions were given little choice but to fight. The strike had long antecedents but the new Conservative government took up the battle with a determination to see it through to the bitter end. SIM had never before been involved in industrial conflict on this scale.

The strike began as Grundy was on the verge of leaving and Draper was to take over as Acting Senior Chaplain during an 18-month interregnum before the arrival of Mike West. David Lunn, the new Bishop of Sheffield, had not yet arrived, and it fell to the Suffragan Bishop of Doncaster, Stewart Cross, later Bishop of Blackburn, to support the chaplains through the dispute. Draper had worked in Brown Bayleys under Stokes' supervision before his ordination. He then moved to Sheffield as curate with the Manor team, before becoming a full-time member of the Mission staff in 1978. He was determined not to be a mere caretaker, but to continue to improve links with local Churches, to raise the significance of unemployment in the Mission, and to develop lay discipleship.

But the steel strike dominated the first few months of 1980. Because it had been a long time in the brewing chaplains were prepared, and were well informed about the issues and the motives involved in the strike. They used this information to mount a major publicity campaign within the Churches. They wrote to 600 clergy in the mainstream denominations throughout South Yorkshire explaining the issues, challenging prejudice and media stereotyping with factual information, and asking for prayers for all involved. They preached and spoke to many Church meetings.

The morning the strike broke the chaplains went to their respective works. Gordon Wilson, for example, spent the morning with the pickets at British Steel Stainless. He then asked to be allowed through the lines to visit management. "Why not?" they said, "You can't do any harm, and you may do some good." Inside he was briefed on the view of the BSC Board, and also saw the frustration of local management. They had been used to conducting industrial relations themselves and now everything was controlled from London.

As well as visiting pickets and management, Grundy and Draper kept in close contact with the union's strike headquarters in Sheffield and Rotherham respectively. To maintain visible impartiality Draper would visit both the strikers' and management's headquarters on the same day. SIM was not a negotiator or go-between, it was pastor to people caught up in conflict. Strict confidentiality was observed with all the parties. Nationally, through the Industrial Mission Association's Steel Chaplains' Network, chaplains met BSC's chief executive, Bob Scholey, to state their anxiety for the industry as a whole, and their particular concern at the proposed complete closure of plants in Corby and Shotton.

SIM also had to deal with the media. The initial letter to local clergy had also been sent to the press and, with a photograph of Wilson warming his hands on a pickets' brazier, it had received a surprising degree of coverage. In caring for all chaplains also had to work hard to avoid co-option by either side. This was no easy policy and it provoked frequent misunderstanding, a difficulty that was magnified in dealings with the press. In an interview on BBC Radio's "Sunday" programme, Grundy was repeatedly pushed to say that the chaplains sided with the pickets. He was told by journalists, however, that only one newspaper had deliberately set out to misunderstand the Mission's position – *The Church Times*.

The strike lasted 12 weeks and the work force was defeated. SIM, perhaps alone, came out well. Each side regarded it as friend. In Rotherham, Draper's meticulous work meant that a chaplain was welcomed back into the Templeborough mini-mill, previously Steel, Peech and Tozer, for the first time since the disputes of 1966.[12] The mood had changed in the Church too. Critical voices were few, and SIM did not have to defend its action. Instead it was praised both for its work with those in the strike, and for keeping the Church well informed. Stewart Cross, Bishop of Doncaster, publicly commended SIM for their involvement in a contentious political issue and for successfully walking the fine line between the opposing sides.[13]

The strike, and the defeat of the unions, was a symbolic watershed for industry, industrial policy, and for the place of Sheffield Industrial Mission. The end of the 1970s had contained the first hints that the steel and engineering industries were in decline; the early 1980s confirmed it. Unemployment was rising. The cyclical pattern of boom and bust in the steel industry ended; closed steel works were physically razed and the jobs lost forever. Consensus politics was derided by the Conservative government and industrial democracy was buried. Works councils collapsed in the strike and were not re-convened. The industrial culture SIM had shared and the ideals it had espoused were swept away, along with many of the firms and the workers whom it had served for 36 years.

This did not happen overnight. After the strike chaplains returned to works visiting. They still had a role in apprentice training. But a conference on "Industrial Conflict and the Christian Faith", planned for September 1980, was cancelled through lack of interest. An open letter on forgiveness went down well with the Churches, but not in the works where many felt bitterly betrayed, not least by the refusal of the clerical staff unions in the industry to support the strike.

Nor did the Mission change suddenly. Chaplains acknowledged that Christian social theology which desired peace but ignored conflict was naive and inadequate. The Mission had relied on, and had reinforced, the ethos of consensus. Industrial conflict was not unusual, but there had been an underlying assumption that all people of goodwill were ultimately aiming at the same goals. For the first time the Mission had to face the reality of fundamental conflicts of interest, and of divergent social goals which would not be reconciled through rational discussion and goodwill. There was also an awareness that, on occasions, it might be necessary for Christians to engage in conflict on the side of justice.

Practical matters also required attention. David Lunn was enthroned as Bishop of Sheffield in February 1980. He expressed some uncertainty as to the role of the Mission's Advisory Committee. Finances were not strong. The team was larger than ever, but could not meet all the requests for chaplaincies. No chaplain had visited Firth Brown, for example, for more than a year when the firm announced 1,200 redundancies. Draper worked hard to increase the number of part-time chaplains, especially in the Rotherham area. He also continued the work of ensuring that the Mission was understood and welcomed by local Churches, giving talks and leading training courses in a wide range of Churches and Church groups.

Unemployment was a particular concern for Raymond Draper, and although not all his colleagues shared this preoccupation, it made an ever increasing claim on the attention of the Mission. Wilson continued Grundy's involvement with Workshop 6, and Nash began work with Sheffield Starting Point, an MSC funded training scheme for unemployed young people. Draper was involved with courses for the unemployed in Rotherham, and in negotiations for a Church unemployment officer in the Dearne Valley. The Mission received a number of requests for help from BSC managers who were losing their jobs, and they reissued their leaflet on facing up to redundancy. In the summer of 1981 SIM and the MSC jointly sponsored a "Churches Unemployment Workshop" inviting Church members concerned about unemployment to explore what practical responses they could make, whether through MSC schemes or in other ways.

The experience of the steel strike had also sharpened a recurrent theme of industrial mission, the difficulty of nurturing lay discipleship. To address what he termed "social discipleship" Draper proposed a "college without walls", a lay institute without the encumbrance of a building. It would redress the Mission's continued failure to enable lay Christians to become more effective disciples in work and society. It would develop a theology, an ethic, and a spirituality appropriate to the challenges faced by lay Christians. It would also contribute to the rediscovery by the Church of its social role. However the immediate response was not enthusiastic and the proposal was not seriously pursued.

It was, however, clear that new industrial circumstances would demand new responses from the Mission. A start had been made, but it would be left to Mike West to oversee the search for a new role.

NOTES

1. *Fox News*, 11.2.71 (the house newspaper of Samuel Fox & Co.)

2. "Industrial Mission – what we are trying to do and why", Minutes of a talk and discussion, ESC Management Group, 5.3.69; and also, "The Industrial Mission", *Dormer Outlook*, No 45, spring 1971 (the house magazine of Sheffield Twist Drill & Steel Co.)

3. *Working with God*, Andrew Stokes, Mowbray, 1992, pp.41-42.

4. "Senior Chaplain's Review of some salient features of past 5 years, for the Industrial Mission Advisory Committee", Andrew Stokes, July 1974

5. Interview with Malcolm Grundy

6. *Report of the Committee of Inquiry on Industrial Democracy*, Chairman Lord Bullock, Cmnd. 6706, HMSO, 1977.

7. *The Church and Industrial Society – a continuing debate*, Sheffield Industrial Mission, 1977

8. *Britain Today and Tomorrow – World Justice and British Economic Priorities*, A study by Sheffield Industrial Mission for the British Council of Churches and Christian Aid, September 1977, p.1

9. *ibid.*, p.12

10. *ibid.*, p.14

11. Letter to Malcolm Grundy on the winding up of the Director's Group, 1979

12. Draper was later able to invite Michael Jackson for a visit to the works symbolising the final healing of these old wounds.

13. in, *The Sheffield Morning Telegraph*, 23.1.80; and also in, *News from the Diocese of Sheffield*, February 1980

5

JUSTICE AND INTEGRITY

Steel and heavy engineering, which had been the air the Mission breathed, seemed to crumble away through the 1980s. Nationally and locally the political rules were re-written. The challenge faced by the new Senior Chaplain, Mike West, was to fashion new methods of mission adequate to the rapidly changing industrial and social culture of the 1980s.

Central government pursued an aggressive monetarist economic policy and they proclaimed with evangelical fervour a political ideology fundamentally opposed to the trades unions, collective action, and socialism in all its guises. Industry was thrown into uncertainty. The first half of the decade saw a rapid and deep recession led by the collapse of manufacturing industry. The second half saw an economic boom led by consumer spending and rapid rises in property values. The recession hit South Yorkshire hard; the boom arrived half-heartedly. With the end of mass employment in heavy industry working-class culture expired largely unlamented. And to hasten the extinction of what had come to be perceived as lumbering industrial dinosaurs came the "enterprise culture": dynamic, individualist, brash, greedy, and, for a brief moment, highly successful for many who jumped on board.

Local politics also changed. The Conservative government set out to emasculate local authorities through legislation and financial controls. Sheffield City Council responded in the first half of the 1980s by high profile political opposition, and in the second half by growing more introspective and less doctrinaire, and by seeking new alliances to recover from the economic devastation the area had experienced.

Mike West was the first Senior Chaplain to come from outwith the ranks of existing chaplains. He had been an industrial chaplain for twelve years, and Senior Chaplain of the Hertfordshire and Bedfordshire Industrial Mission. Amongst other things he brought a more managerial style to staff development. He set himself three initial objectives: to build a more coherent team, to encourage greater openness to developments in industrial mission outside Sheffield, and to improve the professionalism of the work.

West also brought a national and an international perspective from active involvement in the Industrial Mission Association, and participation in the European Contact Group on Church and Industry. This was a dimension of industrial mission work that had not been a large part of SIM in the 1970s, but which was to become increasingly important as the 1980s progressed.

Internationally there had been significant developments in the thinking of Urban and Industrial Mission (UIM) in the preceding two decades. Following its 1961 Assembly at New Delhi, the WCC created a Division of World Mission and Evangelism. This in turn established a UIM programme in 1965.[1] The first Advisory Group meeting was dominated by SIM. It met near the retirement home of Bishop Hunter who was co-opted for the meeting. Wickham was ill and the meeting was chaired by Philip Bloy, representing Africa. Wickham was elected Chairman of the Committee for its first five years.

Fundamentally different relationships between Churches and the industrial power structures were visible at this first meeting. Hunter argued that mission must include getting into the factories. Yet in many parts of the world Christian activists were not allowed through the factory gates. It was a difference between UIM and industrial mission that grew rapidly more pronounced after Wickham ceased to chair the UIM Advisory Committee in 1970.

UIM was a network of several hundred projects in every continent, yet despite its diversity it developed a common ethos.[2] The heart of UIM spirituality was the conviction that Christ was to be found in the poor. Mission was the action of sharing in the life and the struggles of the poor, and thus to be with Christ in his suffering. The authentic Church was realised through this action. Salvation lay in the eradication of the tangible evils of political and economic oppression. In contrast to the Anglican desire to minister to everyone, UIM asserted that not only was it possible for a Christian to take sides, but that to side with the poor against the powerful was an essential element of Christian faith. UIM projects worked alongside the poor in their daily struggle against injustice, or were comprised of the poor themselves. They did not act from a position of power. Action against oppression was not the application of the Gospel, it was the nature of faith itself. Faith was thus automatically in conflict with the secular powers. With this commitment UIM aimed at nothing less than "setting a fundamental challenge to the sentiments, structures and practices of the entire [global] church."[3]

Western industrial mission was included in this political and theological indictment. European industrial mission was seen as politically and ecclesiastically compliant. Even where it worked for social justice, its association with managers, and its dependence on management for permission to enter factories, was seen to compromise the mission to shop floor workers. The assumption that change could be achieved by moral pressure on powerful individuals was dismissed as hollow. From the perspective of Christians working with people in poverty, including those suffering from the commercial practices of western companies, industrial mission evinced little active concern for issues of justice.

These issues were to become increasingly salient in Sheffield as political polarisation grew and as the chaplains and the Churches became more politicised. But West's immediate priority was to address the internal organisational structure for the Mission. SIM had, in effect, been a personal demesne of the Anglican Bishop of Sheffield, accountable only to him. Grundy had begun to explore possible ecumenical structures, and in January 1983 the Bishop's Advisory Committee on Industrial Mission was replaced by an ecumenical Industrial Mission Council. SIM had a formal constitution for the first time. It became a registered charity and a Local Ecumenical Project, accountable to seven denominational authorities through their appointed representatives on the Council. Management and trades union membership was continued, and efforts were made to ensure representation from across the county.

Anglican influence and preoccupations remained strong, but the ecumenical nature of the mission was reinforced by the long-term secondment of staff from the Methodist (from 1974) and United Reformed Churches (from 1978), and by the appointment of part-time chaplains from the Salvation Army, Roman Catholic, and Baptist Churches. These denominations, along with the Society of Friends, were represented on the Council. Not without pride the Mission placed on its letterhead the statement that it "works on behalf of the major Christian denominations in South Yorkshire".

The Council was the structure by which Churches gave the chaplains authority to act as missionaries on their behalf. It was concerned with strategy, with the boundaries of the Mission's work, with formal relations between SIM and the denominations, and with finance. Full-time staff still largely determined the policies and day-to-day practice of the Mission, but through the 1980s the Council became steadily more closely involved in the workings of the Mission, and clearer about its control of the chaplains' activities.

The new constitution stated the aims of the Sheffield Industrial Mission, albeit phrased with an eye to the legal requirements of charitable status.

"The object of the Mission is the advancement of the Christian religion in all aspects of working life including industry, commerce, trade unions and organisations dealing with employment and training for employment in South Yorkshire and to endeavour to increase the understanding of industry and industrial society by the Churches and vice versa."[4]

A new structure, and the challenge of the rapid decline in the steel industry, necessitated a re-examination of the goals and methods the mission. In 1982 West circulated a paper, "The Development of Sheffield Industrial Mission",[5] which argued that the purpose of the Mission had always been to work for change in society in the direction of justice, participation, and sustainability. To be effective chaplains had to improve their proficiency in theology and ethics. However, the lodgement chaplains already enjoyed in industry gave them unique opportunities to apply their expertise. The large questions of morality and society were a normal part of chaplaincy. If chaplains were better trained and could demonstrate the practical relevance of their skills, they could offer companies specific assistance on such matters as industrial relations or the employment of minorities. In particular West proposed that the team learn and implement an approach known as "Doing Theology", borrowed from the theologian Ian Frazer. This integrated ethical issues in an iterative cycle of participation, reflection, evaluation, and so back to deeper participation.

Within the Mission debate on the paper focused less on what West was proposing, and more on what was missing. Pastoral work seemed denigrated to the point of disappearing; and evangelism was accorded no place in either the history or the future of the Mission. The pastoral and evangelistic approach which had characterised the Mission for the previous 15 years, was contrasted with a new emphasis on prophetic and teaching ministry. West was calling for a significant reorientation of the mission. The paper was accepted by staff and Council but only partially implemented in part because the change of ethos it envisaged was too great, and in part because chaplains were not able to change their relationship with companies to be able to offer the consultancy style assistance West had envisaged.

Three years later, in 1985, West circulated another discussion paper to staff and Council. "A Strategy for Sheffield Industrial Mission" looked at the content of the Mission's work in relation to its goal. West defined the goal of the mission as, "the embodiment of Christian values in the relationships, methods and goals of industry and commerce".[6] This aim accepted the world as it was, but only as a starting point. It assumed the practical possibility of visible steps towards Christendom, and it left open to debate the ultimate shape and character of a Christian society. West divided the activities of the chaplains into three: works visiting and associated work with trades unions and employers' organisations; work with local Churches; and projects. At issue was how to move effectively from what the Mission did towards its goal.

This formulation of the Mission's aim immediately begged the questions of precisely which Christian values it wished to embody in industry, and what power the Mission had or could acquire to effect change. While West affirmed the position that chaplains could not claim divine authority to tell industry what to do, he also wanted to find practical means of influencing industry. Discussion was inconclusive.

Acceptance of this paper entailed a change of emphasis in the work of the full-time chaplains. West wished to develop work with lay groups and local Churches that was more systematically targeted on promoting involvement in the industrial and economic world. He wished to give more time to projects, which were defined as having specific goals, a limited life, an identified membership, some of whom were Christians, and using the method of "Doing Theology". He also proposed a new development: that the Church, and thus the Mission, might work with, and even establish, pressure groups which campaigned for change.

These two papers encapsulated and furthered the new path the Mission was following. Chaplains became increasingly aware of political issues, and more tightly focused on questions of justice and inequity in industry and society. But in practice these were trends, not a revolution, and were followed with more enthusiasm by some staff than by others. Pastoral work continued to be important, and the evangelistic emphasis declined as some of the chaplains who had joined the Mission under its previous regime decided to leave. Staff began to see their ministries more as prophetic, though most weight was placed on an incremental, even technocratic, improvement in industry and society. There was also a slow trend for SIM's culture to move from a disparate collection of chaplains engaged in separate activities to a more unified team in which individual ministries furthered the aims of the Mission as a whole. This was reinforced by the presence of an office, first in Tinsley, and from 1985 in Sheffield, which became a common working base for the chaplains.

In 1981 Mike West had inherited a strong and experienced team of eight full- and half-time chaplains, and a network of 18 part-time chaplains. Between them they visited 30 companies and 39 work sites. There was a steady turn over of staff, particularly of part-time chaplains, and the number of part-time chaplains grew throughout the 1980s. Relations between them and the Mission were structured more systematically. Negotiation of entry into companies, transfers from retiring chaplains to their successors, induction into the chaplaincy, continued training, and general support, all of which had been the Senior Chaplain's responsibility, were now shared with more of the full-time chaplains. By the mid-1980s part-time chaplains were undertaking the bulk of the Mission's works visiting. Full-time staff increasingly turned their attention to other activities.

Nevertheless works visiting continued to be the staple of the Mission's activities. The precipitate decline of steel manufacture and engineering had threatened to leave the chaplains with nowhere to go. The Mission responded to this urgent challenge with a revaluation of the place and function of works visiting. West argued that as the object of mission was to effect change in industry in the pursuit of justice, the shop-floor was the place where the tensions and contradictions of industrial society were most clearly visible, sometimes painfully so. Furthermore the credibility of the Mission's movement into other areas of work rested on the intimate knowledge of industry and its tensions that came only from regular visiting. Works visiting thus remained central and necessary for the Mission, but it was no longer either sufficient or normative. It was demoted to be one method amongst several to achieve the Mission's goal of social change.

West reinforced the centrality of works visiting by widening the range of industrial and commercial undertakings which had chaplaincies. New chaplaincies were developed in companies or sectors of employment which were major employers or which had strategic value to the Mission in the pursuit of its objective of social change. The choice was limited by pragmatic considerations which excluded, for example, civil service departments who were major employers but, as Malcolm Grundy had found in his discussions with the Manpower Services Commission, chaplains would not be permitted unfettered access to civil servants in their offices. The process of diversification, however, was slow and steel and engineering chaplaincies continued to dominate the Mission's portfolio.

The Mission placed a new significance on chaplaincy in the retail, leisure, and high-technology industries because these were perceived to be the key new employers replacing the old, metal based industries. Retail chaplaincies were extended beyond those already undertaken by Elizabeth Nash. A Methodist lay worker, Tony Brookes, initiated chaplaincies in a number of stores in Doncaster town centre. However, a careful study in 1988-89 of the possibilities of a chaplain to the leisure sector, or to the vast new shopping complex at Meadowhall, came to nothing; priority was to be given to economic development issues in the same district. What did happen was that certain chaplaincies which had been undertaken by parish clergy and others outside the mission (notably to some football clubs and stores in the centre of Sheffield) came slowly under SIM's wing. SIM initiated a chaplaincy in the Sheffield Science Park in 1987. This was a new area of work and it showed that chaplaincy to very small firms was possible, at least where they were clustered under one roof.

The most significant development in works chaplaincy during this decade was with the South Yorkshire Fire and Rescue Service. In 1984 the Chief Fire Officer approached SIM seeking a chaplain. He wanted a full-time chaplain who would offer his staff pastoral care. The mission could not commit a single individual, and it was also concerned to ensure that any chaplain would be permitted to raise wider issues about the Service, and would not simply be expected to bless fire engines. Negotiations with the unions focused on the potential role of a chaplain in an industrial dispute.

The Fire Service offered particular challenges to the Mission. It was strictly hierarchical in organisation, and fire-fighting teams functioned in tight-knit, almost family groups. It was decided to assign chaplains according to a pattern which broadly matched the structure of the Service. As the Fire Service covered Barnsley, in the Anglican Diocese of Wakefield, SIM had for the first time to recruit chaplains from outside the borders of the Diocese of Sheffield. A full-time member of staff, initially Gordon Wilson, provided a chaplaincy service at County Headquarters, and kept contact with senior Fire Service staff. Chaplains were recruited for the divisional headquarters and the sub-stations as there were people available. Supervision, training, and regular meetings with management were arranged on an industry basis. An annual review of the whole chaplaincy was undertaken by the Chief Fire Officer and, in the first years, representatives of each of the unions. In their stations chaplains worked hard to be accepted as one of the "family" whilst also being honorary members of the officers' club. Pastoral care of fire crews, and on occasions members of the public, was the largest part of the work. Chaplains could be called out to attend a major incident. On rare occasions staff were referred to the chaplain for counselling as an alternative to disciplinary action. Political issues might also be raised, including equal opportunities. In an overwhelmingly white, male service the recruitment of black people and women was an issue of sharp debate.

The most difficult places to be a chaplain in the 1980s were the traditional areas of steel and engineering. Redundancies and closures were pandemic. A constant sense of vulnerability became the daily bread of industrial chaplaincy. Chaplains desperately wanted to console workers and managers trapped in circumstances beyond everyone's control. They shared the anger of those being discarded and encouraged those fighting to save their jobs and, it seemed, their industries. They consciously, and at times simultaneously, gave two contradictory messages of hope: look to redundancy as an opportunity, and fight hard for the job you've got. Sometimes they could offer practical help; more often they could only stand and watch. Some reflected ruefully on the difficulty of counselling those facing possible redundancy, given their own security of employment with the Church.

In such interesting times regular visiting, chatting, and listening provided a framework which could, and did, lead in remarkably diverse directions. Chaplains struggled with people facing moral dilemmas at work; took up issues of health and safety; visited the sick; counselled those suffering from stress; and occasionally took the funerals of people killed at work. Steve Hoggar, a Methodist full-time chaplain responsible for Sheffield Forgemasters, found himself supporting senior managers charged with illegally exporting tubes to Iraq for a "Supergun". Another chaplain was asked to exorcise parts of a factory; another led informal services of worship in the work place conference room. When BSC Special Steels in Stocksbridge passed into the private company United Engineering Steels on April 1st 1986 a service was held in Stocksbridge Church to mark the occasion. A local radio station rang to ask whether praying for the prosperity of the steel industry was an April fool joke. All that was asked of chaplains, and the opportunities that were open to them, came as a consequence of their sustained commitment to the companies and their employees.

Nowhere was this more clear than in the Hillsborough football disaster. More than 90 Liverpool fans were killed through crushing and asphyxiation. Gordon Wilson had been chaplain to Sheffield Wednesday since 1979. His early days with the team had not been propitious. Team manager Jack Charlton had invited Wilson to visit and look round. During this initial visit Charlton precipitantly announced on Radio Sheffield that Wilson was to be the team's chaplain. The news was picked up by *The Daily Mail*. The Methodist hierarchy thus discovered the appointment through the media, to the particular chagrin of the local minister who had been trying for two years to land the job. It was not an easy place to visit and to strike up relationships partly because managers changed, and partly because Wilson was seen to have been imposed from on top. Nor was it initially an official SIM chaplaincy. In 1979 it was regarded as something of a perk, less serious than the real steel-focused ministry, and it was several years before the chaplaincy was accepted as a formal part of SIM.

On the afternoon of April 14th 1989 Wilson heard the news of the disaster on the radio. He went straight to the ground. For the rest of that week he spent every waking hour there. As chaplain to both Sheffield Wednesday and the Fire Service he played a key role in the emergency operation and in the days afterwards. He was given complete authority to act on behalf of the Club in matters relating to counselling. He had to negotiate with the Social Services, the Police, denominational authorities and others to ensure that all worked smoothly together. On one occasion he threw an ITN crew out of the grounds. He offered counselling and support to those away from the limelight, the ground staff and others, who were equally deeply affected by the tragedy. He worked closely with the West Midlands Police investigating the tragedy. He participated in the memorial services held in Sheffield and Liverpool Cathedrals. The Church would have been involved in any case, and many clergy gave hours comforting and counselling the bereaved, but such intensity of work was only possible on the basis of the relationships that had been built up over ten years' chaplaincy to Sheffield Wednesday.

Long term chaplaincy also led the Mission to become involved in industrial action. The Mission had had a chaplaincy at the Tinsley Park plant of BSC Special Steels since its opening in 1960; in 1985 its closure was threatened. Led by Clifford Auckland, who had been chaplain to the works for the previous five years, the Mission joined the joint trades union campaign, though at arm's length, in a fight to save the plant. The plant's defenders argued that closure would seriously damage the industry and be a major blow to the economy of both Sheffield and Rotherham. The Mission's contribution to the campaign was a carefully researched leaflet arguing against closure. They circulated it to the local industrial and political community, as well as to the Churches, and to national organisations.

The highly public action of the chaplains attracted considerable criticism inside the Mission. The Chairman of the Council, industrialist Peter Lee, questioned the chaplains' ability to comment on technical questions. He felt they had not listened to arguments for closure; he disagreed with chaplains taking sides so publicly on such a controversial issue; and he asserted that their role was to minister to all in industry, which could only be damaged by such a public and partisan stance.[7] There were other criticisms too: that the level of analysis was superficial, and the tone of the leaflet was unchristian – the text was measured; the cartoons were biting. Peter Lee's critique, and the more cautious view of chaplaincy on which it was based, were not shared by everyone on the Council. Nonetheless the Council was agreed that the chaplains had exceeded their authority in joining the campaign without prior agreement with them.

When the dust settled, with the campaign lost, it was evident that SIM had gained respect amongst trades unionists. One sign of this was that chaplains were then asked to supervise and count two union ballots. Local management too had valued the Mission's intervention: they had felt as distant as the unions from British Steel's decision making that affected them so closely.

The Mission played a significant, interventionist, but more discrete role in a second industrial dispute. In 1984 Sheffield Forgemasters had been created through a merger of Firth Brown and the River Don Works of British Steel. It was never an easy alliance given previous rivalry between the constituent firms, different management styles and expectations, separate union structures, and varying terms and conditions of employment. Gordon Wilson was relatively new to the firm and relations with senior management were not strong when a strike broke out in late 1985 triggered by the dismissal of two trades-union convenors. The strike was further embittered when 700 workers were sacked. Management threatened to wind up the company. Neither side was speaking to the other.

In this bleak atmosphere Wilson was approached by one of the people at the centre of the dispute and became pivotal in breaking the stalemate. With Mike West, the Anglican Bishop of Sheffield, David Lunn, and the Roman Catholic Bishop of Hallam, Gerald Moverley, he worked carefully to clear the ground between the disputants and to bring both sides to the point where the formal involvement of the arbitration service, ACAS, could be effective. The task was made more sensitive by the apparent involvement of the Prime Minister's office in the course and resolution of the dispute. In Wilson's view the terms of the final settlement were almost wholly those that he had put forward, apart from the word "convenor" which was removed from the agreement, apparently on Mrs Thatcher's personal insistence. Forgemasters was no longer to have full-time paid trades-union officials.

On another occasion the Mission actively supported Michael Keen, the Anglican Diocesan Unemployment Officer, in the campaign to keep open a glassworks at Swinton, outside Rotherham. Keen developed the innovative tactic of contacting a number of Christians in South and South-East England, whom he knew through the Christians' Unemployment Group, to persuade them to lobby their Conservative Members of Parliament to endorse the campaign. The support of local Labour MPs was guaranteed and ineffectual. When the battle was lost Keen organised a service in the village church as an occasion on which the people of Swinton could publicly and collectively symbolise both their bereavement, and also their commitment to the future.

The second strand of the Mission's programme, alongside works visiting, was its links with Churches. These had never been entirely satisfactory. Chaplains continued to be extensively involved in local Church life through preaching and teaching and in the governance of their denominations. Yet industrial mission and local congregations had very different foci, priorities, understanding, and spirituality, and the gap between them remained as unbridgeable as it had ever been. The 1989 Annual Report contrasted the welcome for SIM in industry, commerce and government, with the attitude of the Churches,

"Sadly local and regional church bodies appear less enthusiastic. They seldom invite contributions from SIM, perhaps because the economy does not appear on their agendas. Some even question the need for a specialised ministry to the industrial and commercial world, or at least a marked reluctance to pay for it!"[8]

SIM determined to improve this relationship, and throughout the 1980s it strove hard to put its association with local Churches and lay Christians onto a systematic and purposeful basis. In 1985 West envisaged that chaplains might act as tutors or facilitators to Church-based lay groups to encourage their participation in the industrial and economic world. There were few takers. Other approaches were tried. SIM built a network of liaison people across many Churches; staff preached extensively; part-time chaplains were encouraged to reflect on the connection between their industrial and other ministries. In 1988 chaplains offered to preach if this could be combined with an evening study session. Take-up was small, and even those congregations which invited a chaplain generally preferred preaching without study.

Regular contact was maintained with lay people in the Churches and in industry through the publication of a free quarterly news sheet *Lookout!* from 1984.[9] This publicised changes in the staff, gave an insight into the activities and concerns of the Mission, and highlighted ethical or industrial issues with which the chaplains were grappling. It had a print run of 3-4,000 copies.

Chaplains continued to provide training aimed variously at lay people, ordinands, and clergy. They led Lent groups, which were popular, but (by definition) they stopped at Easter and did not lead to continuing work. The summer student course continued. Each year around 15 ordinands were given an introduction to the industries of the region and the work of industrial mission. A course called "Theology at Work" was started in 1987 and ran for several years. It comprised four full day sessions in the spring, with a project to be completed by the autumn under the supervision of a member of the Mission staff. Each year "Theology at Work" took a different theme and attracted about half a dozen lay and ordained students. The Mission twice tried to convene informal lunch-time meetings aimed at those working in Sheffield City Centre. On both occasions it was poorly attended and petered out.

The most adventurous initiative in work with lay people was the launch of a membership scheme in September 1987. It was designed to improve links between SIM, Churches, industry and commerce; to provide a pool of people willing to participate in the work of the Mission; and to help chaplains learn how better to support lay people at work. Membership would also generate new income for the Mission. The launch was unpropitious: embarrassingly few came to the capacious reception rooms in Sheffield Town Hall. Recruitment was slow and it became evident that people joined to show their support for the Mission, and as an alternative to active participation.

Through the energy it put into relations with local Churches the Mission was able to build connections systematically, but chaplains were not then able to capitalise on these links in the purposeful way they hoped. They could not evoke or create Christian discipleship in the public arena, though they could offer support and even training to Christians already concerned about such issues. Perhaps they failed because they were attempting to incorporate lay people into their own enterprise which was essentially clerical, or because they were hoping to implant their own, missionary, culture into the very different priorities of local congregations.

The third dimension of the Mission's activity was the development of "projects". "A Strategy for Sheffield Industrial Mission" defined projects as collaborative work with specified goals, a limited life, an identified membership, some of whom would be Christians, and work which used the methods of "Doing Theology". In fact the term disguised an untidy rag-bag of activities. Projects were not new in themselves, for example, every Senior Chaplain since Michael Jackson had been actively concerned with issues of racism and black workers. What was new was that projects now became part of the core of industrial mission work, and were given equal status with works visiting in the canon of the Mission's methods.

Projects were highly diverse. They included a half-day conference on unemployment; active participation in MSC schemes responding to youth unemployment; a study of Christian responses to information technology; participation in secular bodies such as the local Council for Racial Equality and the Low Pay Campaign; and a parish-based group which examined practical alternatives to paid employment. Projects were not study groups but were means by which practical if small steps could be taken towards greater justice in society.

One project was a link with Sweden. In 1979 John Thompson, who could speak a little Swedish, had been the driver for a group organised by the Diocesan Youth Officer. From this initial contact grew a programme of exchange visits between SIM and the Church and Working Life officers of the Diocese of Vsteras which took place every other year between 1981 and 1987. In turn these connections led to a parallel programme of visits between Rotherham Trades Union Council and the Swedish Metalworkers' Union which took place between 1984 and 1989.

Another, long-term project was the "Working Women's Group". This was a group of low-paid women initially brought together in 1985 by a German trainee pastor on placement with SIM, Ulrike Schmidt. The group stayed together after her departure, supported by Elizabeth Nash and Molly Kenyon and, later, Margaret Halsey. They attended the Kirchentag in Frankfurt in 1987. The group met monthly, sharing experience, Bible study and studies on other topics including the WCC programme, "Women in Economic Justice".

Friendship and regular meeting over a long period engendered a mutual openness and trust. Common experience became essential elements of a shared spiritual journey: low pay, shift work, familial and domestic expectations, sexual harassment, all became food for spiritual growth. The acceptance that their own stories were of value in their spiritual explorations contrasted with conventional patterns of spiritual development which sought to constrict spiritual exploration in pre-existent and ill-fitting moulds. Nash argued that the Gospel demand was for everyone to become a full person in their own right. Yet the Church, like the world at large, overvalued men and their experience and devalued the experience of women.

"A theology which continually holds before it the importance of women, instead of disregarding them, would be a new theology indeed. A Church without women is unthinkable, but a Church which truly values them would be very different."[10]

There were a number of tangible products from projects. Some of those which focused on unemployment fed into practical initiatives; a slim leaflet on information technology was produced; an exhibition was mounted in Sheffield Town Hall showing the international links of local companies. But the greater significance of projects for the Mission lay less in what they produced than in the scope and legitimation they gave chaplains to experiment and innovate. The very diversity of projects revealed blind alleys, addressed new areas of work, and suggested novel approaches to mission.

One major aspect of project work was the involvement of chaplains with other organisations, over and above their links with trades unions and employers' associations which arose as a consequence of works visiting. "A Strategy for Sheffield Industrial Mission" had suggested that chaplains might join pressure groups which campaigned for greater justice. Joint work took place with a range of groups: Christian lay groups, campaign groups, and statutory and voluntary groups concerned for the welfare of the region.

In joining other groups chaplains acted both as individuals and as representatives of the Church. Consequently such work also carried an implied message about the relationship of the Church to secular organisations. As it had been since Hunter's day, the Labour movement was politically dominant in South Yorkshire, and much joint work was undertaken with organisations and individuals who were themselves part of or sympathetic to the Labour movement. In the 1980s some on the left regarded the Church, not without surprise, as one of the few consistent critics of Thatcherite ideology and all its works. Trades unionists welcomed the Church as an ally, for example on the People's March for Jobs or in the campaign against the closure of Tinsley Park Works. Other sections of the Labour movement continued to regard the Church with abiding suspicion as an integral component of the Establishment, antagonistic to the claims of working people. Nash worked with the Low Pay Unit for several years before she felt she was accepted as expressing the genuine concern of the Churches for low-paid workers. On the other hand Industry Year 1986 showed that business too welcomed the approval of the Church.

Joint work with Christian lay people was most extensive in addressing unemployment. Chaplains continued to be heavily involved with schemes for young unemployed people sponsored by the Manpower Services Commission. Gordon Wilson became a director of Workshop 6, and Elizabeth Nash chaired Sheffield Starting Point until the MSC's changing rules and priorities led to its demise in the mid-1980s. Attitudes to involvement with the MSC were mixed. The Mission examined the possibility of sponsoring a county-wide MSC scheme; at another point they decided to eschew any further involvement with MSC, and to explore alternative methods of working with the unemployed. In fact both approaches continued side by side.

Away from MSC-funded schemes innovative and creative work was being undertaken with and for unemployed people by the Christians' Unemployment Group, ChUG, and by the Diocesan Unemployment Officer, Michael Keen. The Mission was closely involved in initiating both areas of work, but was not directly responsible for either.

ChUG[11] had been born from a conference jointly sponsored by SIM and the MSC in 1981 (see above, p. 93). Thirty people joined at the inaugural conference. By 1988 it had over 200 members, and seven groups meeting throughout South Yorkshire. ChUG's aims were to turn Christian concern about unemployment into practical action. They worked to help unemployed people in practical ways, and campaigned to promote an awareness of unemployment in both the Churches and the wider community. But from the beginning ChUG was primarily a network of prayer.

Prayer was not simply a private exercise. Prayer vigils were held around the county. They were often led by Church dignitaries, sometimes with the support of civic leaders. The local media was interested and bemused. Unemployment Sunday was instigated by ChUG and later converted to an annual, national observance through Church Action with the Unemployed (CAWTU). An *Unemployment Worship Book* was published by the Sheffield branch.[12]

ChUG was not a political organisation and it claimed to contain a wide range of political views. Yet to be apolitical was not to be politically inert. Members actively lobbied the Prime Minister, the Bishops in the House of Lords, and Rotherham Borough Council, calling for a better deal for the unemployed. With others it campaigned successfully to keep open a Job Centre in Sheffield that had been threatened with closure. Other practical action included the establishment of a holiday fund in Rotherham, enabling unemployed people to take a holiday, often for the first time in many years. In Conisbrough ChUG member Jane Thomas worked with others to set up the Highway Project. A house was renovated in the centre of the village in which unemployed people could come together to gain skills, a social life, and self-confidence. Practical action stemmed directly from the theological conviction that unemployment was an evil.

ChUG was very largely Raymond Draper's creation and he continued as its Chairman on leaving the Mission to become Rector of Wickersley. Chaplains continued to play an active role in the organisation as individual members and supporters, but organisationally ChUG was entirely independent of SIM.

The relationship between SIM and Michael Keen was more complex. For several years Malcolm Grundy had tried and failed to find the funds to appoint a full-time unemployment worker in the Dearne Valley. Raymond Draper had continued the search. In November 1981 the Diocese of Sheffield had agreed to fund an Unemployment Officer, and Michael Keen was appointed in 1982. He worked primarily in the Dearne Valley, an area of pit villages with very high unemployment split between Rotherham, Doncaster, and Barnsley Metropolitan Districts. Keen participated as a member of the SIM staff, but was accountable to the Diocese through other structures.

Keen's work complemented that of ChUG.[13] He worked with local churches and others to initiate a number of projects under the umbrella title of "The Dearne Valley Venture". Among the first was Thurnscoe Sight and Sound Music Workshop. This was based in the back of what had been a Methodist chapel and it was launched with financial support from the Methodist Church. The Workshop attracted many young people: one group had the chance of a tour of Eastern Europe but had to turn it down because they could not afford transport to take them. Other groups flourished: a print workshop called "Outlook", a community arts workshop, knitting groups, a nearly-new clothes store, basic literacy teaching, a tool library, advice services, and a local history project.

Each project was largely autonomous and developed according to the inclinations and wishes of its members, and the opportunities available. All shared the same ethos: they were shoe-string projects, not tied to the MSC but self-directed. They provided unemployed people the opportunity for social contact, for self-confidence and the chance to develop skills in settings that were neither officious nor patronising, but which accepted each person as important in their own right. Each project was an effective parable of hope in the face of exclusion, dereliction, and despair. Cortonwood in the Dearne Valley had been the flash point for the 1984-85 miners strike. After the strike British Coal turned its back on the community, physically razing the colliery. A small group turned part of the Methodist church into a small cafe and provided meals on a cost basis. They named it Cortonwood Comeback.

The ethos of the groups reflected Keen's theology. He argued that Christian thinking was out of kilter with the created order.[14] Along with people, he said, it was "things", material objects, which made life bearable. Yet much of Christianity was too often abstract and disengaged from the physical world. Christian thought has traditionally extracted a kernel of precepts, propositions, and arguments from the Bible, and has discarded as the husk the stories and objects which carry the meaning. For Keen, one consequence of a right relationship with the physical world was an emphasis on enabling unemployed people to work together making, creating, and restoring things. Projects that worked in this way both carried and revealed something of the meaning of the Gospel; the people in them and the things that they created became signs of God's Kingdom.

Alongside Keen's work with the unemployed SIM was concerned for local economic regeneration, in large part because economic revival implied the creation of new jobs. At the same time it wished to address the patterns of employment which the new employers, in the service sector, brought with them. Male, manual, full-time jobs would increasingly give way to female, skilled, and part-time jobs. These trends were not new, but they were given an added intensity by the speed of the collapse of manufacturing industry in the early 1980s, and the urgent search to attract new service sector employers to the region. Accordingly SIM decided on an experimental post to address this constellation of issues. In 1986 an Employment Issues Worker was appointed.[15] It was new in that it was entirely focused on collaborative work with other agencies, in particular Sheffield City Council's Department of Employment and Economic Development, and it had no works visiting. The Worker was expected to address the local economy of Sheffield as an entity.

In Sheffield local politics was in a state of flux. The City's civic and business leaders had for many years sustained a relationship of sterile antagonism. In the early 1980s, shocked by the speed of decline of traditional industries, both determined that new, urgent, and cooperative measures were needed. A formal partnership was established anchored on the City Council and the Chamber of Commerce, and centred in the Sheffield Economic Regeneration Committee (SERC). SERC was an alliance of most of Sheffield's major institutions. The Churches were not partners[16] but the Employment Issues Worker was present, representing the Sheffield Council for Racial Equality.

This was a new role for an industrial chaplain. It involved representing the interests of the Council for Racial Equality, and lobbying for the interests of black and ethnic minority groups in the City. In turn it meant keeping these groups fully informed about economic developments. The role expanded to encompass more of Sheffield's voluntary sector concerns in relation to economic development. The Employment Issues Worker was not merely an observer, but a participant in local policy making, albeit peripheral to the mainsprings of local power. It was the Mission's first formal approach to local politics since the Frontier groups of the late 1950s.

The announcement in 1988 that a Development Corporation would be located in Sheffield's Lower Don Valley[17] raised considerable local anxieties. Some of the Anglican and Methodist ministers serving the area, along with other voluntary groups, prepared submissions as part of a threat formally to challenge the announcement of the Corporation. They argued as pastors and citizens first that the welfare of local residents might be harmed and should be enhanced; and second, that democracy would be diminished by the imposition of an unelected Development Corporation, and they wished to see openness of decision making in matters which affected local people. The threat was withdrawn when the City Council negotiated an agreement with the Development Corporation, part of which addressed local residents' concerns.

The group was subsequently expanded under the title "Christians and the UDC". It was primarily a route for information about developments in the Valley, but it also began to examine a Christian framework to evaluate the Development Corporation and its effects. This framework drew together biblical principles and patterns, a pastoral concern for the lives of all those living around the Valley, and factual analysis of the Development

Corporation's achievements.[18] However, after initial enthusiasm, the group was not sustained and the framework was not followed through for the life of the UDC.

The Mission's involvement in local policy making, and thus in the political realm, largely developed in an opportunistic, *ad hoc* manner. SIM's involvement exposed both the absence of the Church from local politics, and the lack of discussion about Christian political thought within the Churches. Christian involvement, however, needed to be based on a foundation of Christian political theology. In practice, this was largely found in the themes of the WCC programme "Justice, Peace, and a Sustainable Society", which both gave a Christian justification to participation in the political realm, and offered signposts to direct that involvement.

Through its collaborative project work the Mission was drawn inexorably further into politics. Simultaneously chaplains were searching for a spiritual understanding of their work, which in turn would be adequate to take them further. Individual chaplains formulated their own approaches. Nevertheless shared experience and challenges led to a common core of ideas and a strong emphasis on the ideals of integrity, wholeness, and mutual respect. In part this was a reaction against the social and personal alienation and disintegration which chaplains perceived around them at all levels. Discipleship therefore was simultaneously a personal, social, theological, political, and spiritual commitment, in the attempt to embody that desired wholeness in oneself.

For Elizabeth Nash each person's whole history was also the account of their salvation. Wholeness for Margaret Halsey lay in the integration of the inner, psychological self and the external person: a division frequently visible as a woman chaplain in a steel works.[19] Michael Keen wanted to restore the importance of the physical world within theological reflection. Tony Attwood, and after him David Walker, worked to build up a parochial ministry in Maltby in which all aspects of the life of the town were integrated. "Doing Theology" sought to bring secular and theological analysis together into a single process with practical action. In 1982 pastoral and prophetic ministries had been contrasted, by the end of the decade they were converging.

By the end of the 1980s West had reshaped SIM. It was a more coherent team, more actively committed to political analysis and action. It was also less uniformly Anglican and more clearly accountable to its sponsoring denominations through the Industrial Mission Council. Links with local congregations were strong, if never adequate. Chaplains played an active role in the Industrial Mission Association and the Mission had re-established its international connections. In Sheffield, notwithstanding the collapse of its traditional industries, works visiting was still extensive. SIM had begun to explore new ways of mission, primarily through collaborative project work. SIM had been set on a new course, moving steadily towards the promotion of justice and peace made tangible in personal, public, and theological integrity.

NOTES

1. See: *A Community of Clowns – Testimonies of People in Urban Rural Mission*, Hugh Lewin, compiler, WCC, 1987. In 1978 the Urban Industrial Mission Desk of the WCC merged with the Rural Agricultural Mission Desk to become Urban Rural Mission (URM). It continued the spiritual and political development of UIM and largely turned its back on British industrial mission.

2. Summarising the ethos of UIM largely from reports of global or regional meetings does violence to the unique insights of each project. Similarly, stories of different projects are susceptible to the temptation of being presented in accordance with the expectations of the audience, perhaps reinforcing common elements at the cost of the differences.

3. *A Community of Clowns, ibid.,* p.xi

4. The Constitution of the Sheffield Industrial Mission, January 1983.

5. "The Development of Sheffield Industrial Mission", M. West, typescript, summer 1982

6. "A Strategy for Sheffield Industrial Mission", M. West, typescript, June 1985. This was an industrial mission objective originating with the Churches Consortium on Industrial Mission, and broadly accepted by most industrial mission teams in the 1970s. Such a formulation had not been included in the constitution of SIM as the lawyers deemed it to conflict with charitable status.

7. Peter Lee, Memo to Council, 23.9.85

8. Annual Report 1989 / *Lookout!*

9. Newsletters had been published at the end of the 1970s but these had appeared irregularly.

10. "Do You Want a Responsible Job?", E. Nash, *Crucible,* January-March 1988, pp.29-36

11. "ChUG, A Story of Unemployment", M. Keen, *Christian Action*, April 1986. *"Fighting Back" A Starter Kit for Christians concerned about Unemployment"*, R. Draper, no publication details [ChUG 1992]

12. *An Unemployment Worship Book*, Sheffield Branch, Christians Unemployment Group, n/d [1987?]

13. South Yorkshire is a small place, and Michael Keen also served as ChUG's General Secretary.

14. "Theology and Unemployment in the Dearne Valley", M. Keen, *Crucible*, October-December 1988, pp.167-173

15. I was myself appointed to this post, half-time, between 1986 and 1990.

16. The Church had, however, played a crucial role in breaking the frozen relationship between City Council and business leaders. A parish priest, Michael Jarratt, had hosted the "Ranmoor Forum", confidential dinners where erstwhile antagonists could explore possible common ground in confidence.
    The Sheffield Council of Churches became a member of SERC in 1988.

17. The Lower Don Valley was a new name for what had been the industrial area of Attercliffe, Brightside, and Darnall. This area had been the geographic centre of SIM's work until the devastation of its industries.

18. "The Sheffield Development Corporation and Central Government Power", P. Bagshaw, *Anvil, for the Diocese of Sheffield*, No. 27, April 1989

19. "Crossing the Boundaries", Margaret Halsey, in *Life Cycles*, M. Halsey & E. Graham (eds.), SPCK, 1993

6

MISSION TO THE COALFIELDS

Of all industry, coal mining has held a particular attraction to missionary minded churches. This may reflect the geographic nature of the industry and the creation of pit villages: built, owned, and exclusively dominated by the industry. In South Yorkshire each village developed its own culture built first on large-scale immigration and then low mobility; teamwork underground; the constant risk and history of shared tragedy; and an underside of slag heaps, violence, and poverty. Until unemployment became the greater threat few miners wanted their sons to follow them underground. The result was a kind of negative social selection: able young people left the area. This geographic and cultural coherence offered Churches opportunities to take a leading role in the community. All the work the Church has undertaken formally with the mining industry in South Yorkshire has had a strong parochial and local Church component.

In 1910, four years before the Diocese of Sheffield was established, the Diocese of York inaugurated the South Yorkshire Coalfield Church Extension Committee[1] which sought to build Churches and to staff them in advance of the insurgence of miners who were to be brought in from other parts of the country to work the new mines. Churches, both new and old, were frequently supported in practical ways by the mine owners. However, in July 1948, the new National Coal Board stopped its contributions, affecting one in five of all Anglican churches in the Diocese. Direct contributions to stipends then amounted to £1,650 p.a., with another £700 in the value of free or reduced price coal. Three clergy houses were owned and maintained by the Coal Board. Some churches and halls were maintained by colliery craftsmen.[2] Bishop Hunter pushed an emergency resolution through the Diocesan Conference opposing the withdrawal of this support, but to no avail.

In that Diocesan Conference debate Hunter argued that the original rationale for the work of the Church Extension Committee had been to provide miners with the resources necessary for their spiritual welfare, much as sports grounds and schools were set up for their physical and intellectual welfare. The NCB gave practical support to these latter facilities, and should do so for the Church in recognition of its continuing contribution to the community. There was, Hunter said, a "quasi-family relationship between

church and industry within one human community".[3] This was special
pleading. From the beginning Churches had been located in mining districts,
with support from mine owners and managers, but they were not churches of
miners.[4] This was true for all denominations.

The Methodist Church was also concerned with the area, addressing it as
a community as alienated from Churches as any in the country. In 1950 the
Methodist Conference set up the "Doncaster District Coalfields Mission" to
undertake a concentrated evangelistic campaign. A variety of methods were
used with some initial success in drawing people into the Churches.
Nonetheless a later review found that their message was most attractive to the
more able young people, many of whom left the area as they grew older.

Contact between SIM and the mining industry through the 1940s and
1950s was patchy. On his arrival in Sheffield Leslie Hunter asked Wickham to
be chaplain to the "Bevin Boys" hostels for workers drafted into the pits
during the war. A number of later contacts led to a weekend conference for
22 miners in 1955.

The first systematic industrial mission work with the mining industry was
opened up by Margaret Kane. As part of her parochial responsibilities at
Maltby she had visited the local colliery, gathered some groups together, and
had participated in the training of apprentices. She continued with this work
on joining the staff of SIM in 1959, concentrating on the Rotherham area.
Her work had two components: to be the missioner to colliers, and also to
encourage Anglican and Methodist clergy to become more involved with their
local pit. For two years she visited underground weekly in Elsecar colliery and
elsewhere, and she continued to build up work with trainees. She convened
six-monthly meetings to which all the local clergy were invited. The creation
of a consistent policy towards the industry, developed across the denominations, was appreciated by the industry. The troubles of the Mission in the
mid-1960s meant it could not be sustained.

Throughout the 1950s Hunter had consistently encouraged work in the
coalfields, exhorting parish clergy to build better links with their colliery.
There were occasional signs of progress, but not enough for Hunter. In the
late 1950s he began talks with Mr W.H. (Bill) Sales, then Chairman of the
Yorkshire Divisional Coal Board.[5] Hunter, sometimes in the company of the
Bishop of Wakefield as Diocesan boundaries did not coincide with those of
the Coal Board, visited several of the local area headquarters. Negotiations
took some two years, but Hunter did not inform SIM until they were
concluded and an appointment made.

In May 1961 Hunter announced that Charles Grice was to be Rector of
Armthorpe parish, with a particular responsibility to build a bridge between

the parish and the local colliery, Markham Main. This was no sinecure. The pit had a reputation for poor industrial relations and a strong communist presence, and there was general agreement that if a relationship could be established there, it could be done anywhere. The ground had been well prepared. Grice had worked for over twelve years as a miner before ordination and he fitted Sales' stipulation that the chaplain should be "competent underground". He had also been a member of the National Union of Mineworkers which helped in establishing good relations with the miners. There was an initial hiccup in negotiations with the local NUM: where should Grice bath and change after a visit? He said he was used to pit-head baths and didn't mind being seen there, to which the union man replied, "That's not the problem. It's thee seeing us that's the problem".[6] Thereafter he showered and changed in the pit's Rescue Station.

In September 1961 Grice was informed that he was to have a curate, Leslie Brooks, who was also to be Missioner to the South Yorkshire Coalfields. Brooks largely took over the direct work with the colliery, working through local organisations associated with the mine, becoming, amongst other things, Secretary to the local Coal Industry Social Welfare Organisation. But the nature of the parish meant that this work could not be kept in a separate box, and Grice was still actively involved in the affairs of the pit.

In 1965 Bishop Taylor asked Grice to extend the work. Still working independently of SIM, he left Armthorpe to become Missioner to the NCB's Doncaster and South Yorkshire areas, and attached to Doncaster Parish Church. The Coal Board paid half his salary and half his expenses; the Church paid the other half.

Grice's work comprised regular visits to collieries, both pit top and underground, and chatting wherever there was an opportunity. In contrast to the Industrial Mission model he did not seek to bring groups together for discussion, in part because the nature of the work made this impractical. There were, however, always natural meeting points where conversation could be superficial or deeply serious. Medical centres and time offices were important points of contact where he would be pointed towards those who were off sick. Pastoral care of the ill, of miners who found it hard to express their anxieties and feelings about work underground, or of young people in trouble, was always important. He was notified of all serious accidents, and might be asked to inform a miner's family of an injury or death. He met local management regularly and this relationship, in particular his relationship with the Area General Manager, affected the extent and nature of his chaplaincy, not least because the Board paid half his salary. On one occasion his work faced a value-for-money review. It survived. Work with apprentices took up an increasing amount of Grice's time. By the end of his post as Missioner to the Coalfields teaching consumed two days a week, and the fee was paid to the Diocese against his salary. He also made sure that he maintained good relationships with local clergy, making it clear that he was complementing their work, not competing with them. Grice's pattern of work was to be the foundation for future mission work in the coalfields.

In 1969 Grice moved to the parish of Tinsley, where he finally became part of the Industrial Mission team as a part-time chaplain. Most of his work with the Coalfields went into abeyance. However Malcolm Grundy, then curate at Doncaster Parish Church, inherited some of the work with apprentices. He took a class of 70 each week at Markham Main, and then a second similar class at Doncaster Technical College. Despite his previous experience of youth work this was starting at the deep end.

Nearly five years later, in January 1974, David Lawrance was appointed as Industrial Chaplain to the Coalfields and a member of the SIM team. He was to stay 11 years with the Mission. Lawrance had been a Bevin boy, but had to undergo further training before being allowed (from 1977) to visit underground unaccompanied. Like Grice he had to negotiate at each pit the scope of his visits, but once established he would visit regularly. He built up a particular relationship with Markham Main and Brodsworth collieries. After a while he would announce his visits with notices at the pit top. Like Grice his ministry focused on the pastoral care of those in the industry and conversations with miners wherever there was an opportunity. He continued to work with apprentices at the Coal Board's training centre, and re-established links with the NUM and local and area Coal Board management.

Lawrance's brief was both to develop work in the collieries himself, and also to encourage local clergy to work with the pit. In the first six months of his appointment he visited all the Anglican clergy in places which could be defined as mining parishes. He judged five clergy (four Anglican and one Methodist) to be effectively connected with their colliery and community. Of these, one saw the pit as the fulcrum of village life; one had strong political ties with the NUM; and one had had long links with the Industrial Mission. The Methodist (Gordon Wilson) visited underground two pits each quarter, and made weekly visits to the medical centre. Another man made regular and frequent visits to each of the pit social clubs in the parish, and this was the extent of his connection.

More instructive were the responses from the 12 clergy disinterested in Lawrance's approach. Four felt work at the pit would be a waste of time, and three were generally supportive of industrial mission but said that their parish responsibilities meant they could not help. One thought that clergy would close their minds to the idea if they were pressed too strongly. Another claimed that the solidarity of the miners militated against church attendance; and another that he would need "a few weeks to consider with his congregation, in prayer, the effects upon his parish work if he was to give regular portions of time to a closer involvement with his pit.".[7] Four of these clergy had been invited by the local colliery management to visit the pit, sometimes repeatedly, and all had declined.

This diversity of attitude and action, vulnerable to change with each new incumbent or local minister, constituted an important part of the background to the attempt to develop systematic work with the industry. The vicar and other clergy personified the Church in an area, and outsiders frequently judged the Church by their actions. In turn, some clergy perceived a lack of consistency of approach from the Church's specialist staff: one incumbent observed to Lawrance that his was the third approach he had had from the Diocese.

In 1984/85 a strike erupted which proved to be a turning point for the industry. It was also a significant challenge both to the Churches and to industrial mission. Industrial relations were already strained, and in 1983 the NUM had applied a ban on overtime work. In March 1984 British Coal announced the precipitate closure of Cortonwood colliery in the Dearne Valley. They ignored the established consultation procedure which was already strained by the overtime ban. The local NUM went on strike which, under the leadership of Arthur Scargill, spread region by region without a national ballot. It split the union. Nottinghamshire workers who refused to strike left the NUM and formed the Union of Democratic Mineworkers. The Bishop of Sheffield, David Lunn, visited Cortonwood colliery in the first fortnight of the strike.

It was quickly evident that opposition to the strikers was as much political as industrial. In 1974 mass action by miners had brought down the Heath Government and in 1981 the threat of action had secured a reversal of earlier pit closure proposals. This time the Government was well prepared and determined to prevent a recurrence of past defeats.[8] Police were used in large numbers to control the pickets, and to defend miners who wished to return to work. There was violence and the threat of violence from both sides.

The response of the Mission was not unified. David Lawrance felt that, without a ballot, the strike was unconstitutional. He saw the dispute in industrial terms and did not wish to emphasise its political dimension. He talked to the miners on the picket lines and, when allowed, he went through the picket to visit management and those undertaking safety and security work. He visited Coal House, Doncaster, the Coal Board's regional headquarters. He faithfully applied the consensual model of chaplaincy that had been built up in the 1970s. There is a tone of sadness in his observation that, after 37 years of nationalisation, the conflict between miners and management still resembled that between the miners and the old mine owners. He avoided taking sides in the dispute, and bemoaned the absence of middle ground in which reconciliation might be explored.

In practical terms Tony Attwood's response to the strike was similar to those of Lawrance. Attwood had first been encouraged by David Lawrance to visit a pit when he was vicar of Elsecar. As team vicar in Maltby and a member of the SIM team he had visited the local colliery weekly for the two years prior to the strike. In July 1983 he had brought all sides of the industry together with the Church for an exhibition and Service of Commemoration and Renewal which recalled the deaths of 27 men in an underground explosion and fire at the pit in 1923. During the strike he continued to visit all the parties involved weekly, sometimes daily. This was often difficult. At one point outside contractors were brought into the pit. Attwood was only permitted to talk to them if chaperoned by a member of management, presumably so that he did not encourage the contractors to respect the picket. He also visited the police. He was vice-chairman of the local Police Liaison Committee which had to deal not only with the tension between local people and local police as a consequence of the strike, but also with the impact of "foreign" police who showed little regard for long-term relationships. At one point Attwood was himself a victim of their tactics, being chased by police dogs from a picket line in the company of the local Member of Parliament. Ever since then he has been known to some as "the fastest vicar in the land".

Where Attwood differed from Lawrance was in his evaluation of the dispute, and of the appropriate Christian response. He began from a position of support for the NUM, and opposition to what he saw as the casual disregard by the Coal Board of the contribution made by every miner and their family to the wealth and welfare of the country. He consciously put a desire for justice and issues of truth above the wish to offer an impartial, universal ministry.[9] Through his visiting he sought to retain goodwill from all sides, while also making his allegiance clear. He saw his role not as helping to calm or initiate debate, but rather to raise questions, and for Attwood the central question was a spiritual and a political one: how was life itself valued?

Attwood's approach was closely tied in with the rest of his parish. He was one of three clergy in a team which put great store on close collaboration with the laity. His ministry in the strike was thus one part of a close-knit parochial response. The Church also gave practical help: the Church Hall at the Church of the Ascension, Maltby, was at one point supplying 300 meals a day. A group of lay people met with the clergy weekly through the strike, prayers were offered, and reports given regularly to the Church Council, though on one occasion a prepared report was not tabled because tensions were thought to be running too high. Funerals, part of Attwood's normal parochial duties, gave him particular opportunities to express his valuation of miners and their contribution to the community.

The difference of emphasis between Attwood and Lawrance symbolised an important difference of view in the Mission. On the one hand there were those, most of whom had been in post since the late 1970s, who sought to avoid an overtly political analysis. On the other there were chaplains who saw political analysis as an essential part of the mission. The difference in their actions was not great; the difference in their understanding of the missionary task was fundamental.

After the strike a group sponsored by the Diocesan Board for Social Responsibility examined the way that Anglican Churches had responded to the challenges of the strike.[10] They found a picture of mining parishes which were not mining congregations, and whose ministries were severely tested in the multiple strains and conflicts of the strike. Many Churches gave practical help, especially food. Clergy sometimes became channels for financial aid. Regular, sustained, and sensitive prayer was offered, often for a swift and just end to the dispute. All sides in the conflict were prayed for. Churches also offered a haven of peace away from the tension, albeit sometimes at the price of excluding any discussion of the strike.

The role of the clergy was fraught with difficulty. Teaching and preaching on the strike was contentious. Many clergy simply avoided the topic, and some congregations much preferred this silence. Some lay people expressed their resentment that clergy were spending time on miners who never came to Church. The review team regretted this attitude. They identified a need for much more consistent teaching and preaching on issues of social ethics. They also encouraged clergy to participate more fully in their communities. This did not imply taking sides, even in such divisive times. Positions of neutrality had been better explained and understood when clergy stood alongside their community in the strike than when they sought to remain aloof, a stance which was usually interpreted as opposition to the miners.

The response of Methodist congregations showed a similar diversity. Some gave generously; others kept their distance. Caution was often fed by an individualist piety and a horror of the violence which seemed to surround the strike. Some congregations stayed silent on the strike to avoid internal conflict.[11]

When the strike ended without a settlement the industry and the communities were left to cope with the aftermath. In the pits management took strong action to prevent intimidation and recrimination. David Lawrance found that visiting required at least as much and perhaps more sensitivity than he had needed during the strike. Lost capacity reduced the need for miners and many applied for redundancy. The programme of pit closures resumed. Cortonwood was shut and every building above ground was flattened.

In 1985 Attwood left Maltby parish to become the Mission's coal industry chaplain in place of David Lawrance who moved to a parish in Wetherby. He continued Lawrance's work, building on his contacts in both the industry and the Churches, continuing regular visiting, pastoral care, and encouraging clergy and ministers to become involved with their local collieries on a systematic basis. Yet Attwood also took two related steps which drew his chaplaincy along a different route from that of his predecessor. He developed an expertise in coal and energy policy; and he was prepared to use that knowledge to campaign for the future of the coal industry when it seemed under threat. In 1989/90, for example, legislation was proposed designed to increase the importation of coal. Attwood briefed the Bishop of Sheffield for his appearance before a House of Lord's Committee on the issue, where he argued that mining communities would be further damaged by the reduction in employment opportunities that would follow the increased importation of coal.

But it was in 1992 that SIM, led by Attwood, engaged in its most extensive campaign. In October that year the President of the Board of Trade, Michael Heseltine, announced the closure of 31 out of the remaining 50 pits. In South Yorkshire this would leave only three functioning pits. The resultant outrage – expressed in the Conservative heartlands as well as in Labour dominated mining districts – caught the Government unprepared. Several Conservative back-bench MPs announced their opposition to the Government's decision. In a tactical retreat, the Government decided to review of the decision and bought themselves time.

The announcement of closures had been widely rumoured in the industry. Attwood had already raised the issue at the Adwick-le-Street Deanery Synod in Doncaster where he was rural dean; he had briefed the Bishop of Sheffield; and he had circulated information through the Industrial Mission Association. Approximately a week before the announcement he had issued a press release to the Church papers, and to some of the local and national media, setting out the likely impact on the communities of the anticipated closures.

On the day of the announcement the Bishop's Council was meeting in Sheffield. On its unanimous recommendation the South Yorkshire Ecumenical Council circulated to all Churches in the area a petition which asked for a review and reversal of the closure plan. 70,000 people signed it. Christians were asked to write to their Member of Parliament and directly to the Government. Churches, particularly those in mining areas, were urged to join a protest rally in London. This Church response was unprecedented. For the first time on an industrial issue and a specific item of Government policy there was overwhelming agreement amongst Church leaders and lay people that they should protest as Christians opposing a perceived injustice. Few voices were raised against the involvement of the Church in politics.

The announcement that the closure decision would be reviewed meant that there was time to organise a strong campaign to keep the pits open, and also time for gut-level opposition to dissipate. During the winter of 1992/3 SIM set about campaigning, and keeping the issue at the front of the Churches' agenda.

Campaigning was targeted precisely at those few people who were both accessible and who could sway the Government: discontented Conservative MPs. The Mission wrote to each Church leader of the mainstream denominations whose Member of Parliament was a member of the Conservative Coal group. They sent background information and asked them to lobby their MP to vote against the Government. A high percentage of the leaders wrote or spoke to their MP, and many also expressed their appreciation of the Mission's contribution. At the same time other private and semi-public lobbying was being undertaken at all levels. In October 1992 the Coalfields Chaplains' Network had a long-arranged meeting with the Minister for Coal, Tim Eggar. They used it to press their arguments; he responded by explaining the realities of the market for coal as the Government saw them. The two discourses never met.

The Church campaigners were making a number of arguments. First and foremost was the feeling that the Government had taken no account of the human impact of their policies. Attwood and others close to the issues argued for a long-term energy policy, in which coal played an increased part, with greater emphasis placed on clean coal technology and energy conservation. Finally, recognising that the closure of pits through exhaustion was a necessity, they called for increased aid to communities affected by closures. A minor theme was the waste of investment, technology, and the remaining coal lost when pits were closed prematurely. These pragmatic arguments were grounded in a Christian belief in the need to value those affected by Government policy, and in the proper stewardship of resources. Yet in practice pragmatic and Christian arguments were elided: which was stressed depended on which was thought to be most appropriate to the audience.

A more general approach was required to keep the issue high on the Churches' agenda. In October 1992 the Mission had convened a meeting of all clergy from the South Yorkshire coalfield area and it met monthly through this period. Nationally, SIM rapidly built links with a wide range of Church groups in mining areas for mutual encouragement and co-ordinated action. The Sheffield District of the Methodist Church, with clergy in Notting-hamshire, issued a glossy "Pit Closure Action Pack". This set out background and factual information which argued against closure, and also a dialogue and prayers for worship. It contained a list of "Ten things you can do" which mingled political lobbying, local action, and suggestions for worship and prayer.

A national Coalfields Churches Conference was convened in January 1993.[12] By coincidence one of the key political actors was a local Member of Parliament. Richard Caborn MP was then Chair of the House of Commons Select Committee which shadowed the affairs of the Department of Trade and Industry. He spoke to the Conference which then endorsed the Select Committee's conclusions. Its report was published that same week. This envisaged some reduction in the number of collieries, and it identified ways by which the anticipated market for coal could be increased. It was unashamedly an attempt to identify the maximum output which could be politically acceptable to the Government and the Conference backed it on those pragmatic grounds.

In the end the campaign was ineffective. The steam had gone out of the national campaign and through 1993 there was a steady trickle of pit closure announcements which brought the Government and British Coal back to the position they had announced in October 1992.

Nevertheless the dispute had exposed a sea-change in the relationship of the Churches to their political role. On this one issue, based more on gut-reaction than on articulate political critique, and with a stance that was clearly popular amongst people from a wide range of political viewpoints, the Churches had acted in concert to try to change Government policy, using all the techniques of an external pressure group. Their capacity to do so had been greatly enhanced by the expertise of the coalfields chaplains, and also by the organisational and political abilities of the Industrial Mission team working together. But the contribution of Industrial Mission in South Yorkshire was only possible because Church leaders and Church congregations, shared the political will to campaign.

NOTES

1. *A History of the Diocese of Sheffield, 1914-1979,* Mary Walton, Sheffield Diocesan Board of Finance, 1981, pp.6-8

2. *Sheffield Diocesan Review,* July 1948, Vol. 1, No. 7

3. *ibid.*

4. There had been a quite different relationship. Robin Woods cites a churchwarden who "recalled the days when the pit-owners would punish the misdemeanours of a collier – such a serious offence, for example, as being found with matches in his pocket – with compulsory attendance at church for three or more Sundays running." *An autobiography,* R. Woods, SCM Press, 1986, p.123

5. Sales was later a member of the Church of England Industry Committee, and, later still, was convicted for his part in the Poulson scandal.

6. Interview with Charles Grice.

7. Report to the Bishop's Industrial Mission Advisory Committee, 9.7.74

8. Few, however, were then aware of the extent of the Government's preparation for the strike. See, *One of Us,* Hugo Young, 1991; final edition 1993, Pan Books, pp.366-78

9. "Theology under Ambush, a local industrial mission view of some aspects of the United Kingdom 1984-5 Coal Strike", A.N. Attwood, unpublished typescript, 16.4.85

10. *The Church in the Mining Communities – a reflection on the experiences of parishes in the Diocese of Sheffield during the Mining Dispute 1984/5,* Diocese of Sheffield Social Responsibility Committee, 1988. The review team included Tony Attwood and Mike West.

11. *The Coal Strike, Christian Reflections on the Miners' Struggle,* B. Jenner, New City, Sheffield, 1986

12. The conference was convened by SIM, Church Action on Poverty, the Industrial Mission Association's Coalfield Chaplains' Network, and the Diocese of Sheffield's Social Responsibility Committee.

7

INDUSTRIAL MISSION IN SOUTH YORKSHIRE

The Mission began the new decade with a new name. At its 1990 Annual General Meeting it became the "Industrial Mission in South Yorkshire" (IMSY), more accurately reflecting its area of work. It continued to adapt and to explore, though it retained its roots in works visiting in the steel and engineering industries.

In March 1991 there were seven full- and half-time members of staff, and 28 part-time chaplains. Approximately two-thirds of its chaplaincies were still in steel manufacture, engineering, and other metal-based companies. There was a full time Coal Chaplain, and five chaplains visited Fire Service establishments. Of the seven retail and distribution chaplaincies, five were vacant at this point. Trebor Bassett, Sheffield Wednesday Football Club, Sheffield Science Park, and Workshop 6 Training Centre made up the rest. Relations with part-time chaplains continued to be made more formal. In 1992 induction and review procedures were made more rigorous, partly to offer more support to the part-time chaplains concerned, and partly to integrate this aspect of their ministry more closely into both the life of the local church and the work of the Mission as a whole.

Finances were on a stable footing, with a small loss or surplus each year. The largest expense, salaries, was wholly met by the Churches. Companies contributed only around 10% of the Mission's running costs, the remainder coming from congregations, trusts, including the Church Burgesses, and Members. A little under 20% of running costs was generated by interest payments and the Mission's own activities.

Much stayed the same in the Mission's calendar. It continued the summer courses for ordinands, and the Theology at Work courses. Links with local congregations still defied the Mission's aspirations. In 1993 it took the initiative, approaching Churches where it wished to preach and participate, rather than waiting for Churches to come to it.

Project work continued, though more sharply targeted on issues of social justice. Elizabeth Nash continued to work with the Yorkshire and Humberside Low Pay Campaign, and Margaret Halsey undertook a study of the consequences of compulsory competitive tendering of public services, and in particular its effect on low-paid women workers. West's involvement with the

Sheffield Campaign Against Racism led the Mission, with the support of its Council, into an active campaign against alleged racism in a major Sheffield city centre store, Cole Brothers, part of the John Lewis Partnership. The Church's contribution to this campaign was publicly led by the Bishop of Sheffield, David Lunn. The store's chaplains, first Gordon Lacey and then Christopher Smith, continued to visit. Though they were in a very difficult position, they were on occasions able to raise the issues within the store. The Mission supported the Keep Sunday Special campaign, not so much for religious reasons as on the grounds of the detrimental effects on employees if retail stores were widely permitted to open on Sundays.

There were a number of new developments across the range of the Mission's work. After 24 years Barry Parker returned to the team as a part-time, non-stipendiary member. He drew together a group as part of a project to examine transport issues. It had a particular focus on the conflicts of interests between car users, pedestrians and public transport provision; and between pollution and the comforts and quality of life.

In Doncaster Norman Young was appointed in May 1992 as chaplain to the local economy, and half-time parish priest at Barnaby Dun. Doncaster had always been peripheral to the Mission's vision. David Lawrance and Tony Attwood both lived there and the oversight and encouragement of industrial visiting in Doncaster had been part of their brief. There had been a trickle of part-time chaplains through the 1970s, slowly increasing in the 1980s, but Young's appointment was the first focused directly on the Borough.

Through the 1980s Doncaster had seen a rapid rise of unemployment and the progressive loss of jobs in its primary employer, the coal industry. For each job lost in the mine, further jobs were lost amongst local suppliers and services. In the late 1980s a partnership was built between the local Council, private sector bodies and trades unions to tackle the economic regeneration of the town. In this context an ecumenical Town Centre Churches Group had been convened by the Anglican Bishop of Doncaster in 1988 to enable the Churches to respond to the developing partnership in the town. It made a considerable contribution to the debate on the shape of the new Industrial Mission job. In the end the possibility of a job primarily focused on works visiting was rejected, and it was decided that the post should be concerned with the economy of Doncaster as a whole. Young worked to involve local Churches in the processes of regeneration, especially in training and new employment opportunities. He was invited to attend the civic partnership meetings as an observer. He was also expected to develop works chaplaincy in the area.

In Sheffield it was clear that the high profile retail and office developments and the sports facilities newly built in the Lower Don Valley (see above, p.111-112) were not creating sufficient jobs, or appropriate jobs, to meet the employment needs of the surrounding communities. With funds from the Church Urban Fund, the Paul Cadbury Trust, and the Diocese of Sheffield IMSY drew up a job description for a worker who would promote local employment, self help groups, and community business in collaboration with local Churches and the local community. In September 1992 a Methodist lay community worker, Chris Sissons, was appointed. This was a community development post and, despite the experience of Michael Keen's work in the Dearne Valley, it marked a new venture for IMSY. It was a logical extension of work done on economic development in the 1980s.

The Mission also, once again, examined its own purpose and priorities. Staff produced a "Mission Statement" that, with a minor revision, was adopted by the Council in February 1992.

INDUSTRIAL MISSION IN SOUTH YORKSHIRE

MISSION STATEMENT

Industrial Mission in South Yorkshire is part of the whole mission of the Church. An ecumenical agency, serving as a link between the world of faith and the world of work, it is committed to:

◆ developing and sustaining diverse forms of Christian presence in the world of work;

◆ sharing in the creation of Christian understandings of economic, social and political issues;

◆ working to promote God's justice in economic and social matters alongside people within and outside the Church;

◆ encouraging the whole Church in South Yorkshire in its engagement with the world of work.

Industrial Mission in South Yorkshire is involved in:

◆ chaplaincies in companies in the industrial, commercial and service sectors;

◆ dialogue with trades unions, management organisations, local government, the voluntary sector;

◆ work alongside local communities, women's groups, black and Asian groups, and others who share a concern for justice and equality;

◆ co-operation with local congregations and other Christian groups seeking to develop the Church's witness in public life;

◆ training for lay people and clergy.

Believing that all people are called to share with God in creation, with Christ in redemption, and with each other in transforming an imperfect world, those who work with *Industrial Mission in South Yorkshire* affirm that:

◆ social and economic structures are means through which people share in God's purpose that creation be fruitful and harmonious;

◆ social and economic structures which destroy the integrity of creation, and which oppress people in body, mind or spirit, run counter to God's purpose and must be opposed;

◆ these structures can and will be transformed, enabling all people to fulfil their potential as human beings, through relationships that reflect the Gospel values of love, justice, and peace.

The contrast with the lay leaders' document of April 1950 (see above, pp. 22–4) can scarcely be exaggerated.

Some concern was expressed by Council members about the effects that this Mission Statement might have on readers in industry. It was the most political of any statement the Mission has made about itself and its aims. For the first time it stressed both a commitment to justice along with a willingness to oppose destructive and oppressive forces. It was also clear about IMSY's willingness to form alliances with those who share their political perspective irrespective of their Christian allegiance. Such a politically charged statement was only possible because the Churches represented on the Industrial Mission Council had themselves become much more politicised.

However, notwithstanding its importance, the political dimension was secondary to the assertion that IMSY was, first and foremost, an ecumenical agency of the Church. It was firmly grounded in both the Christian faith and the Christian Churches. It echoed a changed relationship between the Mission and the world. The concept of a "link between the world of faith and the world of work" replaced the idea that the Mission might constitute a bridge between the Church and industry.

Behind this statement lay a spirituality of Christian discipleship which worked for justice within the present structures, yet which longed for the transformation of those structures. It was universalist, but it put God's justice as its highest value and therefore was prepared to subordinate the values of Christian unity or of ministry to all sectors of society. It reflected a belief in the all-encompassing nature of God's redeeming love, and it remained clear sighted on the need to oppose evil in its daily, practical manifestations. It asserted that everyone would be included in a redemption in this world, a redemption characterised not by an explicit Christianity, but by "the Gospel values of love, justice and peace".

A number of the key ideas of this statement, not least: "the world of faith and the world of work", "social and economic structures" and "justice", were left highly imprecise. But this was a Mission statement. It reflected ideals and aspirations as much as contemporary reality. And it was left to the Council, staff, members, and those associated with the Mission to work out the details in practice in the changing economic, political and social circumstances of the end of the twentieth century.

POSTSCIPT

Holiness in the World

At the heart of Christianity is a paradox: God, who is holy, transcendent, and ineffable, is yet made visible in the flesh and blood of the historical person of Jesus of Nazareth. This paradox is embodied in individual Christian discipleship, and also in the Church as a whole, as both struggle to realise faith in the secular world.

Industrial mission, with one foot in the world of faith and the other in the world of work, has lived out this paradox in a particularly sharp manner.

> "It has been from its beginning ... an extended seminar in applied theology, conducted in an unfamiliar setting (the workplace) and with no guaranteed audience. In the process of clarifying its own mission it has raised issues about the nature of the whole Church in the world."[1]

Industrial mission is an agency of the Church, sent out by the Church into the secular world of industry. Its missionary nature necessarily places it on the boundary of the Church, a location captured in the key images of the "gulf" and the "frontier". The gulf is the divide between the Church and the world; the frontier is the point where Church and world meet. The gulf has to be bridged; the frontier explored. SIM's changing understanding of the nature and purpose of its mission has been visible in the kaleidoscope of ways in which the images of gulf and frontier have been interpreted.

The particular boundary that the Mission straddles is the boundary between the Church and the secular industrial and political order. The Church experiences the paradox of faith in an institutional form. It accepts the modern secular ordering as unquestionably legitimate, although, by definition, its authority and legitimacy are grounded in human structures, while the authority and legitimacy of the Church is God: numinous, infinite, and transcendent. The way these incompatible positions are worked out in practice constitutes the discipleship of the institutional Church in the midst of the institutions of the secular world: the Church in politics. Historically it may be that the Church has experienced this paradox most often as a dilemma, and has sought to resolve it either by a desire to dominate society, or by retreating from it into individualist piety. Yet neither position is tenable for long. In practice there has been a wide variety of relationships, and the border between the Church and the social order has been fluid, imprecise, and unmapped.

This lack of clarity poses a particular problem for industrial chaplains. Although SIM is an agency of the Church, authorised and commissioned by the Church to undertake a particular piece of work in industrial society, in practice chaplains have to a great extent determined their own priorities and working methods. This has meant a constant danger that chaplains might stray across the unmapped border into action unacceptable to the Church, especially when they became involved in industrial conflict or politics. Indeed, the border often only became clear when transgressed. The separation of authority and control constantly raised questions of accountability of SIM to the Church.

In the early 1940s these were distant problems. The initial motivation for the Mission was Hunter's perception of the gulf between the Church and the industrial working class, and the urgency of the challenge this posed the Church. To cross the gulf new techniques were needed which would be appropriate to the depth of the divide. Ted Wickham drew very little from the Churches' earlier approaches to industry because they all, including other examples of works visiting, failed to grasp how great the gulf was, and they glossed over the extent of the challenge to the Church. By contrast he rejected the French worker-priest model partly on the grounds that the gulf in Britain was not as wide as it was in France. Hunter characterised Wickham's approach as "costly identification": to be with the workers on their territory, to drink in their pubs, and to talk about their concerns in their language. Wickham had stepped across the gulf, and showed it was possible for others to follow.

The presence and the depth of the gulf was a particular indictment of the Church of England and its relationship to the industrial order. It had patently failed to be the national Church that it claimed to be. Wickham charged the Church of England with refusing to acknowledge that it occupied merely a narrow niche in the social structure of the country, and that, as a consequence, it held no appeal to the working class. This was not a symptom of decline because the Church had never held the working class. The Church was in fact aligned with and financially dependent on the capitalist class. The depth of the alienation of the Church from the shop floor implied that if Christianity was to be established in the works it could only be done apart from the parochial ordering of the Church of England.

SIM was born at what was both the beginning and the peak of consensus politics, and the ideals of consensus became part of its genetic code. From the beginning SIM stood for justice in industry. But it did so from within a general framework of the affirmation of industry,[2] and only to the extent that it did not offend the sensibilities of management. Where chaplains breached this principle they could be excluded from the works, thus halting the mission.

The development of the Mission reflected the historical circumstances of the steel industry. The social disruption of the war, the sense of common purpose, and the lack of serious industrial conflict, allowed Wickham access to the works. The pattern of steel manufacture – of intense activity and longueurs – gave him opportunities to establish the snap-break meeting and the "Sheffield model" of works visiting. The optimism of the post-war period, as well as his own undoubted charisma and skills, enabled Wickham to build up lay leadership in the works.

Wickham was guided by a classical approach to missions in foreign territory. He immersed himself in the culture and language of industry. The missionary task was to translate the Gospel into the vernacular, and to build up a worshipping church, with an indigenous leadership sufficiently deep rooted in faith to thrive without external oversight. This was a long-term goal, perhaps the work of several generations as other missionary enterprises had been.

By the time he moved to Manchester Wickham had created a new expression of the Church in the works. He had planted the Gospel in new soil so that faith might flourish outside the constricting structures of the dying Church of England. That his creation crumbled cannot be laid at Wickham's door. The missioners he left behind him were inexperienced, but all were committed to furthering the Mission as he had created it. Yet the new para-church was too fragile, its leaders too inexperienced, and the relationship between laity and chaplains too ambiguous, for it to withstand Jackson's unanticipated, and at first unrecognised, change of direction. Nor were there spiritual reserves elsewhere in the Church on which they could draw. Because Wickham had built an alternative to the structures and culture of the Church of England, lay leaders had only the slimmest contact with the hierarchy of the local Church, and Bishop Taylor would not support them. When trouble came the lay leaders turned back to Wickham because their own resources were inadequate and they had nowhere else to go.

Yet precisely because the experiment was stopped by Jackson, and did not collapse on its own account, it is impossible to judge whether it could have succeeded.[3] It leaves a tantalising sense of unfinished business, if only…

For Wickham's successors in 1961-1965 the gulf between the Church and the secular world, and the inability of lay Christians to be effective witnesses in the world, was accepted as an unquestioned fact of life. But SIM's very success, its widespread acceptance in industry and elsewhere, implied that chaplains and the Mission's laity did not themselves share that alienation. Working, as it were, on the other side of the gulf chaplains were able to stress the frontier, the common territory between the Church and the world. Their frontier task was to reconstruct Christian theology in such a way as to support the Mission as a lay enterprise, and to enable the wider Church to be faithful to its calling in the new circumstances of the secular world.

The desire to bridge the gulf between Christianity and secular culture lay at the heart of secular theology. "Demythologising" was the process of rooting out those elements of Christianity which, it seemed, separated modern people from faith. Chaplains both explored secular theology to the point of questioning Christianity's metaphysical base, and simultaneously reasserted a sacramental faith in which God's holiness was perceptible in the most mundane practicalities of ordinary life. However, although the intention may have been to restore the potential for belief and a sense of the holy amongst secularised people, the consequence was to threaten the numinous content and nature of the Christian message.[4]

Michael Jackson's *volte face* abruptly halted radical theological exploration. In its place came a more conventional and more conservative orthodoxy. He rebuilt SIM on a redefinition of the nature of the gulf, a denial of its depth, and a relocation of the Mission in relation to the boundaries of the Church. His erstwhile colleagues had, he believed, both made a virtue of their location in industry apart from the Church and had forgotten that the purpose of mission was to convey the Christian message across the gulf. Jackson's alternative proposal of dialogue and research acknowledged the distance between industry and theology, and suggested a means by which the two could be brought together which did not require the theologian to leave the Church's side of the divide. The new SIM remained on the edge of the church, but firmly anchored to it. Political action was drastically curtailed, discussion of social class largely absent, and the gulf between the Church and industry downplayed. The risk that chaplains might transgress the boundaries of what was acceptable to the Church was thus kept to a minimum. In so far as the Mission was concerned with effecting change in industry it was limited to their influence on individual decision makers.

Despite the assertions of radical critics the new Mission under Andrew Stokes did not seek to "take God into the works": all creation was God's. However, chaplains did assume that consciousness of God, and knowledge of God's truth, lay in the Churches and this they took out to the people. To extend the parochial ministry into the works was to stress the normative importance of the Church in matters of faith and the value of its traditional spiritual disciplines. Chaplains preached the faith by what they said and did, epitomised in Stokes' picture of chaplains as signs of Christ in the hell-like conditions of industry. They also, perhaps initially to their surprise, uncovered faith amongst the unchurched, though the faith they found was often inarticulate and implicit. They condemned their predecessors for so obfuscating their own beliefs that those who had an innate faith could hear only the denial of God.

The Mission's change of direction combined with changing patterns of work in industry to limit the methods open to the Mission. Works visiting remained its staple activity, but works-based meetings of all types were disrupted in 1966, and progressively declined through the 1970s. They were rare by the start of the 1980s. Conferences and student placements declined still more precipitately. New methods, such as Study Days and Lent groups, were largely Church based. Groups of Christian laity in the works proved difficult to sustain.

Under Malcolm Grundy the theological gulf was all but eradicated. There was a single continuous frontier between secular analysis, theological understanding, and the imperatives of Christian discipleship. This worked in both directions. Religious questions could be raised with those in industry through discussion of the underlying values and principles with which they worked. John Thompson's Society of Brother Lawrence promoted the ideal of a seamless continuity of employment and the mystical apprehension of God in the depths of the soul. Conversely, practical responses could be evoked from the Church in regard to unemployment by secular, even statistical, statements of the problem which were also descriptions of the evil, and prescriptions for a Christian response. In so far as there was a gulf for Grundy and for Draper it was the practical one which lay between the crying needs of the unemployed and the inertia of much of society including the Churches.

Throughout the 1970s SIM had given little prominence to political issues. Practical responses to unemployment were portrayed primarily as a Christian moral duty, although it was also direct intervention in a political issue. In the works chaplains continued to promote the central ideas of consensus. Notions of participation, reconciliation, and fairness at work remained constant themes, even when the political consensus that had nurtured these ideas had started to break down. On the one occasion, in 1977, when the Mission systematically asked its industrial contacts for their views on moral aspects of industry[5] it was clear that it was whistling a different tune to that of the industry it served. The general avoidance of a political action did, however, keep SIM in line with the general tenor of the Church.

With the industrial convulsions of the 1980s the Mission embarked on a search for new methods appropriate to new circumstances. Works visiting remained important, but it became one method amongst a number. In particular, the Mission began to develop patterns of collaborative work with a variety of secular organisations. The gulf which gave the Mission a renewed motivation and new direction lay between the Gospel demands for justice and the apparent growth of injustice in secular society. Consequently the Mission became increasingly overtly political. Yet what dominated the Mission's image of itself was not the gulf, but the idea of the frontier, conveyed in the word "links". The Mission saw itself as weaving together many disparate threads into an integrated whole, rather than standing as a bridge over a chasm. The threads it drew together included theology, secular analysis, works visiting, parochial ministry, the institutional Church, the different denominations, secular organisations, and individuals' own experience of life.

The 1980s also saw a sea change in the relationship of the Church to social and industrial issues. This was particularly visible in the Church of England. It felt increasingly obligated to respond to social and political polarisation, and sporadic friction with the Prime Minister, Mrs Thatcher, reinforced a long-term tendency towards greater independence from the State. At the same time there was a growing acceptance of the reality that active membership of the Church of England was confined to a small minority of people. The idea that the Church of England was the national Church, though still present, began to be supplanted by a sense that it was but one denomination amongst many. As such it began to see its interests as perhaps better served by cooperation with other denominations, than by too close an identification with the State.

There was no shortage of political issues which directly impinged on SIM's industrial work, but its capacity to respond in a political manner was steadily increased by the Church's greater acceptance of overtly political views and action. The movement in the Church's stance is revealed in its changing reaction to SIM's involvement in industrial conflict. After the steel strike of 1980 SIM was commended for treading the narrow line between opposing sides; during the 1993 campaign to keep collieries open SIM was commended for providing Church leaders with ammunition to lobby Conservative Members of Parliament to vote against their own government. SIM and the Church had moved together.

With the need for a political theology to underpin their growing involvement in political issues, chaplains turned to liberation theology, particularly as expressed through the World Council of Churches' Urban Rural Movement. Yet only on very rare occasions did SIM's growing emphasis on justice lead it into a straightforwardly confrontational approach to mission.[6] SIM drew from liberation theology the possibility of taking sides in a conflict as Christians, and rejected the requirement to side unreservedly and unambiguously with the oppressed against the powerful as an article of faith.

In fact, against the background of national political polarisation and conflict in the 1980s, SIM remained wedded to the assumptions and values of consensus. It aligned itself with moves towards local political and economic partnerships which brought business and Labour leaders together. Where it became overtly involved in industrial conflict SIM stood "on the side of the industry"; working alongside both management and workers locally in their common fight against a bigger external enemy, whether that be the Government or the recession. The other side of this consensual approach is that SIM has never raised the basic ethical questions of its continued involvement in, and thus its endorsement of, companies which are heavily committed to the armament and nuclear industries.[7] Nor has it raised the environmental consequences of products and processes in the firms it visits, with the one exception of endorsing clean coal technology. Again, this standpoint reflects that of the wider Church. Tension between Church and State in the 1980s partially reflected the fact that the Church remained wedded to the ideal of consensus while the State had rejected it.

After fifty years, has the Mission been a success? No objective answer is possible.[8] SIM's objectives have usually been formulated as ideal goals beyond practical expectation. It has always been dissatisfied with its work with lay people and, apart from some aspects of its first phase, SIM has not effectively been a lay movement. People have come into the Churches through each of the Mission's phases, though there is no way to count them; and the Church has been seen and heard in places from which it would otherwise have been excluded. There is no evidence that industrial culture has been modified by the presence of the Mission, but individuals in industry have consistently valued the chaplains' support and their, sometimes critical, contribution to both their working lives and their Christian discipleship. On occasions, such as at Hillsborough, the foundation that the Mission has laid down through its sustained visiting over many years enabled it to play a significant pastoral and public role.

The results of the "extended seminar in applied theology" lie less in what change the Mission has been able to effect than in its ability to enrich the Church's understanding of discipleship. SIM has consistently grappled with the paradox of faith worked out in the world outside the Church. In doing so it has pieced together the jigsaw of faith, belief, practice, and secular reality.

The result has not been a single picture, nor even a sense of steady progression towards one normative picture, but a sequence of motifs, of different formulations and reformulations of the nature of contemporary discipleship, each of which has contributed unique insights and understandings.

The Mission also has knowledge, ethical reflection, insights, and experience of working with a wide range of secular organisations which can be placed at the service of the Church in its institutional discipleship. However, to the degree that the Church regards its boundaries as sources of threat and alien influence which demand ever vigilant policing, it is unable to accept or to value the insights of the Mission. Where faith is conceived in contrast to secular culture, to be protected against contamination by modernity, the Mission may not be welcome. But to the extent that the Church regards its boundaries as a potential sources of strength and new life, the Mission has much to offer. Where faith is conceived as risk, as working out the paradox anew in the ever-changing world, struggling to keep the temporal and the transcendent together, the Mission may find a welcome.

Since 1944 Sheffield Industrial Mission has bridged the gulf and explored the frontier between the Church and the world. It has contributed to the potential for Christian discipleship in the industrial, commercial, and civic life of South Yorkshire. It has enriched the discipleship of the Church in society. It has sought to discover God at work in God's world and to further God's work in a godless world. It has struggled to perceive the holy in the unholy, to evoke faith in the midst of the secular, to realise the church beyond the Church.

NOTES

1. *Industrial Mission – An Appraisal. The Church's Response to the Changing Industrial Economic Order*. The Report of a working party, commissioned by the Industrial and Economic Affairs Committee of the Church of England's Board for Social Responsibility. BSR, 1988. p.49

2. The Mission saw the development of industry as part of the providence of God. This was not, however, a simple or uncritical affirmation, and the relationship between industry, progress, and providence was complex. See, "Technology and Providence", E.R. Wickham, in *Encounter with Modern Society*, Lutterworth Press, 1964, pp.44-50

3. There must, however, be a presumption of pessimism. No other industrial mission was able to create a self-supporting para-church. See, "Requiem for American Industrial Missions", S. Paradise, *Audenshaw Papers*, No. 41, March 1974

4. It is probable that those who felt most threatened were defenders of traditional orthodoxy, not workers on the shop floor.
   The conflict of 1964-1966, and the revaluation of their predecessors' work by chaplains of a very different persuasion, have made an adequate evaluation of the secular theology approach almost impossible.

5. *Britain Today and Tomorrow – World Justice and British Economic Priorities*, A study by Sheffield Industrial Mission for the British Council of Churches and Christian Aid, September 1977. It is also probable that the managers the Mission talked to were likely to be amongst the more thoughtful and morally aware in industry.

6. Most notably over alleged racism in Cole Brothers.

7. Firms with which the Mission had contact were sometimes invited to bring a product symbolising their industry to the Mission's annual Industry Service. On one occasion no fewer than three stainless steel hip joints were presented, no doubt also symbolising the face which industry wished to turn to the Church.

8. As with the Church at large, there is no agreed yardstick against which SIM can be measured. The Church has seldom made explicit what it wanted the Mission to achieve. Its own stated goals have shifted markedly over 50 years, and have been formulated as ideals and statements of belief, not as benchmarks. Even if such a yardstick could be agreed, there is then no consistent stream of information which would allow one phase of the Mission to be assessed objectively over against another, nor which would allow the Mission to be compared against other patterns of ministry through the same period. Even an ostensibly objective test, the number of people brought into the worshipping Church through the work of the Mission (and there have been some throughout its history), evaporates on closer examination: there may be many influences on that decision, people come and go from the Church, and recruitment for the Church has not been the Mission's objective. Assessment of success is thus to a large degree coloured by the evaluator's own presuppositions. Calls to assess the Mission's success have often been perceived as no more than hostile strikes.

INDEX

Printed by Sheffield Design & Print
Telephone: (0742) 611563

ISBN 0-9522860-0-9